THE COVID-19 FOOD RELIEF PROGRAM IN NEPAL

ASSESSMENT AND LESSONS FOR THE FUTURE

Balkrishna Sharma, Binod Pant, Raju Laudari, Lila Raj Dhakal, Kamal Pande,
Manbar S. Khadka and Rudi Van Dael

JULY 2023

ASIAN DEVELOPMENT BANK

ADB

Contents

Tables/ Figures/Boxes

Government of Nepal
Ministry of Federal Affairs & General Administration
Singhdurbar, Kathmandu

Tel {
4200505
4200299
4200306

Fax No:4200322

Your Ref No.:

Our Ref. No.:

Foreword

The coronavirus disease (COVID-19) pandemic that surged in late 2019 has a profound impact on the world community, including Nepal. The imposition of a strict nationwide lockdown in Nepal for nearly 4 months in fiscal year 2020 crippled economic activities. The poor and vulnerable sections of society were badly affected. To mitigate the adverse effects of this pandemic, the Government of Nepal introduced the National Relief Program (NRP) on 29 March 2020. This program focused on three key areas: (i) tackling health emergencies, (ii) addressing social protection for the poor and vulnerable by providing immediate food relief and employment Support and (iii) providing economic relief measures. The Ministry of Federal Affairs and General Administration MOFAGA played a vital role during the crisis by issuing timely instructions and guidelines to the local levels to streamline measures that had to be taken up, including unconditional food support to identified communities.

The Asian Development Bank (ADB) provided budgetary support to the Government of Nepal to partly finance activities outlined under the NRP. ADB also provided technical assistance to support the Ministry of Finance and the COVID-19 Active Response and Expenditure Support (CARES) Program Steering Committee for timely monitoring and reporting of the progress of various activities under the NRP. This study assessing the effectiveness of the COVID-19 food relief program was carried out in close collaboration with MOFAGA and the local levels under the mandate of the CARES Program Steering Committee. MOFAGA, as one of the CARES Program Steering Committee members, played a crucial role in coordinating and soliciting data and information from the local levels needed for reporting and monitoring COVID-19- related activities. The study has provided very useful policy recommendations for local, provincial, and federal governments to effectively implement such relief measures in times of crisis.

I would like to thank the ADB CARES technical assistance project team for undertaking this important study amid the COVID-19 pandemic. The specific recommendations are well noted, and we look forward to further collaboration with ADB.

Rudra Singh Tamang
Joint Secretary
Ministry of Federal Affairs and General Administration
Government of Nepal
Singhdurbar, Kathmandu

Foreword

The Asian Development Bank (ADB) pledged a countercyclical budgetary support of $250 million to the Government of Nepal as the COVID-19 Active Response and Expenditure Support (CARES) Program. The program aimed to support the government's National Relief Program in dealing with public health emergencies and mitigating the economic and social impacts from the coronavirus disease (COVID-19) pandemic. ADB provided technical assistance (TA) to the government for supporting implementation, monitoring, reporting, and evaluation of the program.

I am pleased to share that The COVID-19 Food Relief Program in Nepal: Assessment and Lessons for the Future has been completed, under the guidance of the Ministry of Federal Affairs and General Administration (MOFAGA). I recall the program steering committee then had mandated the CARES TA team to evaluate procedures of food distribution for poor and vulnerable groups at the local levels, benchmark the lessons learned, and help standardize national norms for food distribution amid disasters, like the COVID-19 pandemic.

The study assesses the impact of national lockdown on food security and the efforts to mitigate the imminent food insecurity crisis. It discusses the process of identifying vulnerable people, food distribution mechanism, risks and challenges faced during the food relief program, private sector coordination, mobilization, and monitoring mechanism. The study also sheds light on the current issues as to how the local levels address cases of gender-based violence and manage resources.

The study suggests some important policy recommendations useful for strengthening similar relief programs in the future. Strengthening database of the poor, marginalized, and vulnerable households and establishing appropriate targeting mechanisms will be crucial toward the effective delivery of relief packages. Mobilizing adequate resources for the disaster management fund, in coordination with the private sector and civil society, will be instrumental in meeting the requisite fund. I firmly believe this study will be important in better designing and implementing relief programs in the event of any future crises.

Finally, I would like to express my sincere gratitude to MOFAGA for this opportunity to review the food relief initiatives through the CARES Program. Let me congratulate Rudi Van Dael, principal social sector specialist and Manbar S. Khadka, senior economics officer, for leading this work. I would also like to thank the CARES Program's Steering Committee for entrusting this study to the CARES TA team. Congratulations to the team for working diligently during the challenging period of the pandemic. ADB is committed to ensuring social protection for poor and vulnerable groups and is willing to support any relevant government initiatives on social protection in the future.

Arnaud Cauchois
Country Director
Nepal Resident Mission
Asian Development Bank

Acknowledgments

The study team would like to extend its gratitude to the Ministry of Finance (MOF) and the Asian Development Bank (ADB) COVID-19 Active Response and Expenditure Support (CARES) Program Steering Committee members for assigning the study to the ADB CARES technical assistance team and providing overall guidance. The team would also like to thank the Ministry of Federal Affairs and General Administration (MOFAGA) for facilitating and supporting the necessary logistics for this study.

In particular, the team would like to express its sincere gratitude to undersecretaries Khim Kunwar, MOF, and Rishi Acharya, MOFAGA; and section officers Rinu Thapaliya and Krishna Prasad Humagai, MOFAGA, for their painstaking support and guidance in conducting this study.

The team would like to thank Rudi Van Dael, unit head, Portfolio Management, ADB Nepal Resident Mission, for commissioning the study within the mandate of the agreed CARES program and supporting the study with the necessary logistics. Sincere thanks go to Manbar Singh Khadka, senior economic officer, ADB, for his continuous guidance and technical backstopping, without which this study would not have been possible. The team also acknowledges the World Food Programme and the United Nations Children's Fund for their inputs in preparing the terms of reference for the study.

Special thanks go to all the concerned local level representatives and staff for the valuable time given to the team despite their busy work schedules. Everyone worked very hard to ensure that the study was conclusive and comprehensive to the extent possible. In addition, the team would like to thank beneficiaries of the food support program, representatives of nongovernment organizations, the media, the Red Cross, and members of *tole* (section of the city) development organizations for sharing their experiences on unconditional food assistance support with the study team.

Abbreviations

ADB	Asian Development Bank
CARES	COVID-19 Active Response and Expenditure Support
CBO	community-based organization
CMIS	Crisis Management Information System
COVID-19	coronavirus disease
FCHV	female community health volunteer
FGD	focus group discussion
GBV	gender-based violence
KII	key informant interview
MOFAGA	Ministry of Federal Affairs and General Administration
NGO	nongovernment organization
PWD	person with disability
SGI	small group interview
TA	technical assistance
TDO	tole development organization

Executive Summary

The global outbreak of the coronavirus disease (COVID-19) pandemic, which began in late 2019, has confronted humanity and civilization with unprecedented challenges. The crisis has harmed hard-won development gains while exacerbating preexisting and chronic issues, including poverty, hunger, and unemployment.

The Government of Nepal announced a nationwide lockdown on 24 March 2020, which affected all social and economic activities in the country. The restrictions were lifted in the summer of 2020, and this was followed by a significant drop in COVID-19 cases. In fiscal year (FY) 2020 (ended July 2020), the economy contracted by 2.1% against the government's target of 8.5% growth. The lockdown adversely affected unorganized occupational groups and migrant laborers, resulting in food insecurity, particularly in urban areas.[1] It created a situation whereby most wage earners, including impoverished and vulnerable households, had no choice but to rely on the government's food assistance program. Local governments, through the ward offices, distributed food to the poor and vulnerable households, including daily wage earners in the informal sector, between 24 March 2020 and 21 July 2020. The Ministry of Federal Affairs and General Administration (MOFAGA) carried out the necessary facilitation and coordination for food relief support.[2]

Following the agreement on the COVID-19 Active Response and Expenditure Support (CARES) Program signed between the Government of Nepal and the Asian Development Bank (ADB), the program Steering Committee mandated the CARES technical assistance (TA) team to prepare a terms of reference document on (i) evaluating or reviewing the procedures followed in distributing relief packages to the poor and vulnerable groups at the local levels; (ii) benchmarking the lessons learned; and (iii) helping standardize national norms for distributing food to the poor and vulnerable groups amid disasters, like the COVID-19 pandemic.

The CARES TA team carried out a study in collaboration with MOFAGA at nine local levels to assess the impacts of the lockdown in terms of food insecurity and efforts made at the local levels in distributing the relief package. The study attempts to comprehend the process of identifying vulnerable people, the food distribution mechanism, the risks and challenges in food distribution, private sector coordination and mobilization, and the monitoring mechanism. Among other things, the study also assesses the status of local-level support in addressing cases of gender-based violence; managing resources, including internal control practices; mobilizing resources for the COVID-19 funding; and evaluating approaches used to monitor the quantity and quality of food, etc.

---

[1] The Sample Relief Standard for Informal Sector Workers and Destitute 2019 of the Ministry of Federal Affairs and General Administration (MOFAGA) defines unorganized occupational groups as follows: porters carrying goods from shops/business stores to home; tourism porters; construction-related porters; porters in hard-to-reach areas (where there is no means of transportation); loaders on trucks, trippers/trucks for carrying construction materials, or vans; agri-laborers who work for daily wages on others' agri-farms; persons working rearing children and persons with disabilities on a daily wage; laborers working in brick factories and brick crushing; masons/carpenters/helpers working for a daily wage; small shopkeepers; magazine sellers in the street; small shopkeepers selling goods on carts or cycles; persons working in others' shops for a daily wage; drivers/helpers who drive others' vans and vehicles; taxi drivers who drive others' taxis/three-wheeler rickshaws in a mutual contract with the owners; rickshaw and cart movers; laborers working in motor garages; laborers working in garments, carpets, tailoring, embroidery, fabricating, etc.; laborers at local level who work for a daily wage.

[2] MOFAGA issued a guiding framework to help local levels implement this program effectively.

The study intended to cover local-level food distribution management from 24 March 2020 to 21 July 2020.[3] It employed a qualitative method to assess the effectiveness of the program implemented across the country. Key informant interviews, small group interviews, and focus group discussions were conducted to assess the methods that local levels had adopted for beneficiary identification, procurement, and food package distribution.

Key Findings

Methods of identifying households eligible for food relief differed from one local level to another. MOFAGA defined vulnerable people under its *Module for Food Relief for Vulnerable and Poor People 2020*. Some provinces also enacted legislation to regulate funds to manage relief work during the lockdown. But the study found that local levels did not follow the guidelines closely, leading to a lack of standardization in the food distribution system. The discrepancies owed mainly to (i) failure to properly review previous policies and regulations before setting new standards, (ii) an emphasis on setting untested standards in an ad hoc manner, and (iii) absence of incorporation of current practices into the module. The selection of beneficiaries was not without flaws, as the selection committee was comprised only of the elected representatives and excluded female community health workers, community-based organizations, women, and social workers.

Addressing specific needs was not common or adequate. MOFAGA issued a circular to all local levels providing the specific nutritious food requirements of pregnant and lactating women, persons with disabilities (PWDs), and people in ill-health. Some local levels addressed these specific needs through their guidelines. However, such people were not adequately represented in the relief program because of a lack of common standards.

A significant amount of COVID-19 funding was utilized for food relief. As per the federal government's guidelines, all local levels established COVID-19 funds to respond to the pandemic. These benefited from the internal resources of local levels; transfers from federal and provincial governments; and contributions from the private sector, international and national nongovernment organizations (NGOs), and individuals. COVID-19 funds were intended for use in various sectors, including health; water, sanitation, and hygiene; quarantine activities; holding centers; and food relief. The study found that the sampled nine local levels had spent 37.2% of the total fund for food relief.

Different procurement methods were applied at the local levels. Local levels were found to have adopted two different approaches for procurement: (i) ward offices purchase food items, following which the municipal office would make payments to these ward offices; and (ii) municipal offices purchase food items and deliver them to respective wards. The primary constraint faced during procurement was that not enough shops were open, depleting food stock at the local levels amid rising prices. Some local levels purchased food items from government-owned enterprises, such as the Food Management and Trade Company and the Salt Trading Corporation, as well as from local cooperatives.

Food quality inspection involved mainly visual observation. Inspection was based only on visual observations of procured food and feedback on food distribution received from beneficiaries. Only one local level conducted a technical quality test of food items through the Food Technology and Quality Control Office. There was no provision for this in the guidelines, but it was a good practice implemented at that particular local level.

---

[3] The field study was carried out during October 2021 to January 2022.

A monitoring and beneficiary feedback mechanism was not institutionalized. While local levels monitored food distribution through field visits and discussions with beneficiaries, a third-party mechanism for monitoring the food distribution process was absent. The study found that, overall, the quality of distributed food was relatively satisfactory at the local levels. However, formal registration, grievance resolution, and feedback practices were generally not in place. Grievances were related primarily to the eligibility of households for food relief support. Local levels tried their best to address such issues by allocating additional food support.

Food distribution information was published on the local level websites. Several local levels prepared food distribution summary reports and published them on their websites. One local level was found to have disclosed ward food relief expenditure. However, local levels generally did not make serious efforts to conduct public or social audits of food relief expenditure.

Coordination and mobilization of the nongovernment sector were fair. The private sector was more interested in contributing directly to the food relief program, whereas international and national NGOs were more interested in providing support from their regular project activities. Overall, coordination by the local levels of the private sector, NGOs, individuals, and civil society in procuring and distributing food to the needy was fair.

There is an institutionalized disaster and pandemic response planning at the local levels. Local levels are guided by the Disaster Risk Reduction and Management Act 2018 with regard to disaster preparedness, response, rescue, and rehabilitation of victims. All local levels had formed disaster management committees and executed the relief program during the COVID-19 crisis effectively. The crisis even saw the formation and operationalization of ward-level disaster management committees for a short time. These committees have a disaster management fund, but this is insufficient to address emergent crises.

Updating of the Crisis Management Information System and its utilization were weak. The Crisis Management Information System (CMIS) data was useful for all three tiers of governments in terms of monitoring the crisis and the relief program. However, local levels are yet to establish an enabling environment for information management or to create dedicated information technology sections in this regard. Further, CMIS data was not fully utilized for planning and policy formulation, including monitoring.

Key Lessons Learned

Despite mobility restrictions amid the COVID-19 pandemic, the Government of Nepal managed its food relief program successfully, with active participation of the local levels and generous support from development partners, NGOs, and the private sector. The Government of Nepal strategically mobilized the private sector during the crisis and succeeded in achieving the desired results—i.e., resource collection, and procurement and distribution of food relief items to the vulnerable groups and the communities. The private sector, individuals, and civil society at the local levels demonstrated their resilience to disasters and extended support to the vulnerable groups and families, complementing government work in food assistance during the pandemic. Local levels were able to successfully identify and manage resources through a "single door"[4] and to provide food relief to people in quarantine, in isolation centers, and in communities on a large scale. They addressed the food insecurity issues of women, children, PWDs, senior citizens, and people from the lowest strata, including unorganized occupational groups.

However, the government will have to strengthen the database of the poor, marginalized, and vulnerable households with disaggregated data to enable systematic intervention through a proper disaster response mechanism. Some progress has been made toward developing institutional structures, policies, and strategies for disaster risk reduction at the federal, provincial, and local levels.

---

4   All food relief aspects were handled through a single entity.

Key Recommendations

- Improve and maintain a data profile of the poor, marginalized, and vulnerable households and establish and operationalize appropriate targeting mechanisms for identifying beneficiaries at the local levels.

- Mobilize adequate resources for a disaster management fund by coordinating with the private sector, NGOs, and civil society.

- Design and implement capacity development (institutional, technical, and managerial) measures for all functional levels, including municipal and ward-level disaster management committees, to enable them to cope with future disasters.

- Explore and adopt alternative means of food support during crisis as per the local context, such as food-for-work, cash-for-work, and cash transfers or cash vouchers.

1. Introduction

The global outbreak of the coronavirus disease (COVID-19) pandemic, which began in late 2019, has confronted humanity and civilization with unprecedented challenges. The pandemic has not been limited to any socioeconomic class, group, or region but spread to 224 countries and territories at an exponential rate. The crisis has negatively affected hard-earned development gains and further exacerbated preexisting and perennial challenges such as poverty, hunger, and unemployment. Nepal's economy contracted by 2.1% in fiscal year (FY) 2020 (ended July 2020) against a growth target of 8.5%.

The Government of Nepal announced a nationwide lockdown on 24 March 2020, which affected all social and economic activities in the country. The restrictions were lifted only in the summer of 2020, and this was followed by a significant drop in COVID-19 cases. The lockdown adversely affected and created food insufficiency for unorganized occupational groups. It created a situation whereby most wage earners, including the impoverished and vulnerable households, had no choice but to rely on the government's food relief program.

Local levels made great efforts to identify those persons or households needing urgent food relief. The Ministry of Federal Affairs and General Administration (MOFAGA) issued a general guiding framework to the local levels to implement the food support distribution program. Local levels devised their own system depending on the local context, the urgency, and the logistics available to support the program within the broader guiding framework issued by MOFAGA. Local levels approached the situation mainly on a case-to-case basis.

The Asian Development Bank (ADB) COVID-19 Active Response and Expenditure Support (CARES) technical assistance (TA) assists the Government of Nepal in monitoring and reporting on progress made under the National Relief Program announced on 29 March 2020 to keep the adverse impacts of COVID-19 to a minimum. One of its activities was to assist in assessing the food relief program and list the lessons learned. The outputs of this study could provide a basis for considering appropriate policy interventions in providing emergency food relief. The CARES TA team carried out the study under the overall guidance of the CARES Steering Committee and in consultation with MOFAGA.

Scope of the Study

The study aimed to assess the local levels' food distribution management implemented during the COVID-19 pandemic, covering the institutional and managerial aspects of food distribution to the poor and vulnerable people in Nepal. It reviewed all applicable policies, procedures, guidelines, and directives.

Out of the total 753 local levels from all seven provinces, nine local levels were selected, taking into account the following: (i) coverage of all provinces, (ii) representation of all local level types, (iii) representation of COVID-19 vulnerability, and (iv) involvement of nonstate actors in relief distribution.

MOFAGA's *Module for Food Relief for Vulnerable and Poor People 2020* guided the definition of eligible households. The main beneficiaries include unorganized occupational groups and destitute persons.[5]

---

[5] Destitute persons refer to individuals requiring help from others to live and homeless people living in the streets, temples, mosques, monasteries, churches, Sikh gurudwaras, old age homes, etc.

Objective

This study's overall objective was to assess the effectiveness of the government's food relief program, including the food distribution mechanism, with a focus on (i) the quality and adequacy of food assistance, with attention to issues such as gender and inclusion, specific needs, participation, risks, vulnerabilities, and the rights of vulnerable groups; and (ii) the resilience of the local levels and their responsiveness to the emergency food situation during COVID-19.

Methodology

The study adopted a qualitative method to assess food distribution and the procedures adopted by the local levels for the identification and selection of beneficiaries, as well as the procurement and distribution of food packages.[6] A quantitative evaluation method was applied to assess the collection of resources from different sources, their use, and the food relief beneficiaries.

Before the commencement of the study, concerned stakeholders, including MOFAGA, reviewed and approved all data collection instruments and the COVID-19 protocol adherence plan.

Data Collection Methods

Document Review

The document review stage included study design, identification of key stakeholders, selection of data collection methods, and sampling of data collection sites. In addition, the study team reviewed information from the websites of the local levels and verified information received from other different sources.

Sampling

The study applied multistage purposive sampling to select municipalities and respondents, ensuring

- representation of all provinces;
- representation of all types of local levels (metropolitan or submetropolitan city, municipality, rural municipality);
- local levels have an average or higher number of beneficiaries among local levels in the district, as per Crisis Management Information System (CMIS) data;
- representation of COVID-19 vulnerability, as per levels of vulnerability (i.e., lowest, low, moderate, high, and highest) defined in the COVID-19 Economic Vulnerability Index report of the Food and Agriculture Organization of the United Nations; and
- involvement of international or national nongovernment organizations (NGOs) in relief distribution in the local levels—COVID-19 Response Tracking Matrix, Who Does What Where, Cluster update from the World Food Programme (as of 25 September 2020).

The team selected local levels and relevant stakeholders for key informant interviews (KIIs), small group interviews (SGIs), and focus group discussions (FGDs) based on the following criteria: (i) key informants from the local levels (e.g., mayors or deputy mayors, chairs or vice-chairs, chief administrative officers); (ii) nine local levels from the seven provinces; and (iii) third-party interviewees such as civil society organizations, NGOs, and the local media as watchdogs regarding food support and the crosscutting theme of gender and social inclusion. Table 1 presents the selection criteria of the local level samples.

Pretesting

Study tools were prepared and pretested in Rambha Rural Municipality of Palpa District in Lumbini Province. Based on the trial result, these were further modified and then used.

---

[6]   The qualitative method consists of a document review, key informant interviews (KIIs), small group interviews (SGIs), and focus group discussions (FGDs).

Table 1: Criteria for Selecting Sample Local Levels

Province	District	Selected Local Level	Vulnerability Index/No. of Beneficiaries/ Partner Engagement/Disasters
Province 1	Morang	Rangeli Municipality	Highest vulnerability; average no. of beneficiaries
Madhesh	Dhanusha	Bideha Municipality	High vulnerability; higher no. of beneficiaries (25,229)
		Janakpurdham Submetropolitan City	To compare outcome with Bideha in same district (decided by study team during field visit)
Bagmati	Makwanpur	Manahari Rural Municipality	Highest vulnerability; ActionAid Nepal supported 148 women
Gandaki	Kaski	Pokhara Metropolitan City	Moderate vulnerability; highest no. of beneficiaries
Lumbini	Palpa	Rambha Rural Municipality	Selected for piloting of instruments; outcome analyzed along with others
	Rupandehi	Suddodhan Rural Municipality	Moderate vulnerability; Voluntary Service Overseas Nepal supported 97 vulnerable households
Karnali	Surkhet	Birendranagar Municipality	Moderate vulnerability; average no. of beneficiaries (23,256); World Food Programme distributed cooked food to 34,338 beneficiaries at transit point
Sudurpaschi	Kailali	Dhangadi Submetropolitan City	Low vulnerability; World Food Programme provided cooked food at transit points to 1,179 individuals

Source: Asian Development Bank (ADB) Project Team.

Key Informant Interviews, Small Group Interviews, and Focus Group Discussions

The study conducted 16 KIIs, 6 SGIs, and 8 FGDs with 86 individuals (of whom 21 were women), including representatives of the local levels, the private sector, media in Nepal, the Red Cross, NGOs, community-based organizations (CBOs), and the beneficiaries (Table 2). The interviews delved into the scope and nature of the challenges in the food relief program, respondents' perspectives on the effectiveness of approaches employed, learnings from past and present efforts, and differential impacts on men and women.

Table 2: Key Informant Interviews, Small Group Interviews, and Focus Group Discussions Conducted

Respondents/Respondent Groups	No. Conducted	Sex Disaggregation of Respondents	
		Male	Female
Mayors/chairs/deputy mayors/vice-chairs/municipal officials	8	29	5
Third party (Nepal Red Cross district chapter, informal sector service center, media, civil society/nongovernment organization, social leaders, etc.)	13	12	2
Relevant selected government officials on service side (Office of Food Technology and Quality Control, Department of Cottage and Small Industries)	1	1	0
Direct beneficiaries and ward-level stakeholders including food distribution center (focus group discussions)	8	23	14
Total	**30**	**65**	**21**

Source: ADB Project Team.

Data Analysis

All the discussion notes were coded under the predefined themes and indicators, and analyses were carried out accordingly. The information received from the different categories of respondents was triangulated to validate it and enhance the credibility of the study findings. The findings, conclusions, and recommendations confirm the objective of the study. All findings were reviewed through a gender and social inclusion lens, with recommendations correspondingly presented.

Limitations of the Study

- The sample size of nine local levels may not fully represent all aspects of the unconditional food support of all 753 municipalities.

- The timing of the study, around 18 months after the program's implementation, means that it may not have captured all relevant data and information.

- The study covers food support by the local levels to human beings only.

2. Findings

Mechanism for Identifying Vulnerable People and Food Distribution

Local levels developed their own criteria for selecting beneficiaries. Only three local levels followed the MOFAGA guidelines. In terms of the procedure followed for the selection of beneficiaries, local levels generally (i) solicited a list of beneficiaries at the ward and/or municipal level; (ii) held discussions with respective ward offices and stakeholders, such as *tole (section of the city)* development organizations (TDOs), mothers' groups, CBOs or NGOs, female community health volunteers (FCHVs), and social workers; and (iii) finalized the list of beneficiaries at the ward and/or municipal level.

Eligibility Criteria for Selection

Five local levels selected beneficiaries by preparing the criteria themselves. Out of these five local levels, three (Bideha, Dhangadi, and Rambha) allowed ward offices to prepare a list of criteria in consensus with the selection committee. Manahari and Pokhara developed selection criteria in line with the MOFAGA guidelines. Two local levels (Rangeli and Suddodhan) did not develop any criteria but asked ward offices to provide a list of people. NGO representatives in Rangeli highlighted that well-off households had also been selected, as a result of political influence, and the number of beneficiaries was also comparatively high. Respondents in Dhangadi stated that the municipality and ward office had developed the selection criteria for food support. The beneficiaries were households of the ultra-poor, persons with disabilities (PWDs), students, and migrants. A team of ward offices was made responsible for selecting the beneficiaries. Table 3 presents the beneficiary selection practices adopted by the sampled local levels.

Beneficiary Selection and Food Distribution Responsibilities

The structure of the COVID-19 coordination committees at the ward and municipal levels and the food distribution process varied from one local level to another. Respondents of Ward 5 of Pokhara said that the ward-level COVID-19 coordination committee and TDOs were responsible for selecting eligible beneficiaries. The poor and vulnerable households were asked to fill up and submit food demand forms. A list of households was collected for TDO recommendation, and then the ward-level COVID-19 coordination committee approved the list with additional screening. In the first stage, 601 households were selected and, in the second stage, 548 households were selected, for a total of 1,149 households.

Similarly, respondents in Dhangadi stated that each ward formed a ward-level COVID-19 management committee consisting of elected officials, party representatives, and members of TDOs. This committee was responsible for the selection of eligible households and the distribution of food relief. In addition, a higher-level committee was formed, chaired by the mayor, to oversee distribution.

Local levels formed committees at the ward level for food distribution. Key informant interview (KII) respondents from Pokhara Ward 5 said they had a 31-member ward-level COVID-19 coordination committee consisting of ward representatives or staff, party representatives, and TDO members. The committee was further mobilized into 10 subgroups that facilitated food distribution. Table 4 presents the responsibility details on beneficiary selection and food relief distribution in the sampled local levels.

Table 3: Criteria for the Selection of Beneficiaries

Local Level	Practices for Selecting Beneficiaries				Remarks
	Ad Hoc Practices	Criteria Developed and Followed		Followed MOFAGA Guideline	
		Ward Level	Municipal Level		
Bideha		✓			List of beneficiaries came from the ward-level committee under the ward chair.
Birendranagar			✓		Local level did not follow the guidelines and standards but made the necessary decisions and followed them accordingly. Survey forms were used in some villages to identify targeted people.
Dhangadi		✓	✓		Submetropolitan city had another committee chaired by the mayor. Food items were also distributed to families that did not receive assistance during the first phase and to highly marginalized families.
Manahari				✓	Ward representatives were mobilized to identify families in difficulty. They also finalized the list following the official guidelines.
Pokhara				✓	Municipal decision, dated 1 April 2020, established the selection criteria in line with the official guidelines, although the local level tried to make them relevant to the local context.
Rambha		✓			Each ward formed a COVID-19 control coordination committee (consisting of elected representatives, party representatives, health persons, and police) responsible for selection of eligible households and distribution of food assistance. It was observed that the participation of all party representatives resulted in a high level of consensus in selection and distribution.
Rangeli	✓				Disaster management committee prepared the list of beneficiaries (9,000 out of 11,000 households).
Suddodhan	✓				Beneficiary recommendation made by *tole* development organization was carried out.

COVID-19 = coronavirus disease, MOFAGA = Ministry of Federal Affairs and General Administration.
Source: ADB Project Team.

Table 4: Beneficiary Selection and Food Distribution Responsibilities

Local Level	Selection Responsibility	Distribution Responsibility
Bideha	Ward-level COVID-19 management committee with elected representatives, all-party representatives, female community health volunteers, teachers, and police personnel	Ward-level COVID-19 management committee
Birendranagar	Local level with recommendation from the ward office based on the list of people identified by TDOs	Ward committee and ward staff with support of TDOs
Dhangadi	Ward-level COVID-19 management committee and committee under the mayor for overall control	Ward-level COVID-19 committee mobilized to distribute food relief
Manahari	Ward-level disaster management committee with elected representatives, police, health personnel, and party representatives	Ward-level disaster management committee
Pokhara	Ward-level COVID-19 management committee with elected representatives, party representatives, and representative of TDO (primarily recommended by the latter)	Ward-level COVID-19 management committee and subgroups
Rambha	Ward-level COVID-19 control coordination committee with elected representatives, party representatives, health persons, and police personnel	Ward-level COVID-19 coordination committee
Rangeli	Municipal taskforce/committee (ward-level all-party structure)	Elected representatives at the ward level
Suddodhan	TDO with the help of the ward-level COVID-19 management committee	Loose committee formed by the local levels consisting of TDO, all-party representatives, and elected officials

COVID-19 = coronavirus disease, TDO = tole development organization.
Source: ADB Project Team.

Types of Food Distribution

Six out of the nine sampled local levels extended their support for both noncooked and cooked food items. Three local levels (Janakpurdham, Pokhara, and Suddodhan) also provided support in cash to buy food. Cooked food items were provided in both quarantine and isolation centers, as well as at community level depending on the situation. KII respondents at the municipal level in Pokhara stated that the local level provided food items rather than cooked food in the initial days of relief distribution. After a couple of months, the municipality also served cooked food or lunch packs to poor and vulnerable households to limit the relief to needy households only. Additionally,

Ward 5 provided cash relief to two families amounting to Nepalese rupees (NRs) 16,000, which was received from an individual donor. Janakpurdham provided NRs300 as cash assistance with food relief items to all beneficiaries to purchase vegetables. Suddodhan provided financial support for buying food to poor families that had lost family members to COVID-19.

Most local levels followed a practical approach in delivering the relief materials to the doorsteps of needy people and families. In rural contexts, agri-laborers were carrying out agricultural activities as usual, with minimum adaptation during the lockdown. Rural communities supported needy people by providing food in kind or by letting them borrow. In urban settings, including transit areas,[7] unorganized groups from different backgrounds faced mobility restrictions, leading to a shortage of suitable jobs matching their skills. They were considered for ongoing support with both cooked and uncooked food because they were at high risk of food scarcity.

Frequency of Food Distribution and Alternatives

Food items distributed to vulnerable people included rice, lentils, oil, and salt. In a few cases, sugar and soap were also provided. Food relief was provided during the lockdown of the first pandemic wave—that is, in early 2020. All the local levels reported that they did not provide food relief during the second wave. The frequency of noncooked food distribution varied from local level to local level, and even from ward level to ward level. Respondents in the Pokhara ward office stated that frequency of food distribution was not consistent

to all households. Households with disabilities were provided food support four or five times, whereas about 30% of targeted households were provided food two to three times.

Respondents in Birendranagar said they had distributed one time but in three stages depending on the category. For example, very poor families received food for a maximum of three times, based on a hotline phone call request. Respondents from the ward office in Birendranagar highlighted that the food package was distributed one time, adequate for about 15 days. Households were categorized as those having four or less members and those with more than four family members. KII respondents in Rangeli mentioned that the food lasted for 15–20 days. Respondents in Bideha and Suddodhan said that distributed food was expected to cover 7–14 days of need. Table 5 presents the type of food distributed to the sampled local levels, and Table 6 shows the frequency of distribution of noncooked food.

Table 5: Types of Food Support in Sampled Local Levels

Local Level	Type of Food Support Distribution			
	Cooked Food	Noncooked Foodstuff	Cash-for-Food	Remarks
Bideha	✓	✓		
Birendranagar	✓	✓		
Dhangadi	✓	✓		
Janakpurdham	✓	✓	✓	NRs300 per family to purchase vegetables
Manahari	✓	✓		
Pokhara	✓	✓	✓	Cash in a very few cases through external donors
Rambha	✓	✓		
Rangeli		✓		
Suddodhan	✓	✓	✓	

NRs = Nepalese rupees.

Source: ADB Project Team.

---

[7] Transit areas refer to where migrants (internal migrants and returnees from India) and vulnerable people were quarantined for some days in holding centers before transferring to their respective districts during lockdown.

Table 6: Frequency of Food Distribution, Noncooked

| | Frequency | | | | Beneficiaries | |
Local Level	Once	Twice	Thrice or More	Remarks	Total No. of Households	No. of Beneficiary Households
Bideha			✓	Ward office distributed food relief thrice (15 kg rice at first and 10 kg later, 3 kg pulses, 2 liters oil, 2 kg sugar, 2 soaps, 1 kg salt, 1 towel, 1 mug, 1 bucket, 5 face masks, slippers in quarantine).	5,817	4,451 (77%)
Birendranagar		✓			23,710	9,647 (41%)
Dhangadi		✓			29,143	10,335 (35%)
Janakpurdham		✓			30,589	15,453 (51%)
Manahari		✓		700 g rice per person per day, 2 kg lentils per family, 1 liter oil per family, 1 kg salt.	7,891	3,370 (43%)
Pokhara				Frequency of distribution not consistent across settlements and municipality did not estimate days to be covered by food packages; however, the local level provided relief in two packages: Full package: 25 kg rice, 1 liter oil, 1 kg salt, 2 kg lentils Half package: 12.5 kg rice, 1 liter oil, 1 kg salt, 1 kg lentils	105,630	20,512 (19%)
Rambha	✓			25 kg rice, 2 liters oil, 2 kg salt, 2 kg lentils	4,626	1,093 (24%)
Rangeli		✓		Local levels requested local donors for high-risk households.	11,249	9,659 (86%)
Suddodhan	✓			25 kg rice, 2 liters oil, 2 kg salt, 2 kg lentils	6,145	4,225 (69%)
Total					**224,800**	**78,745 (35%)**

g = gram, kg = kilogram.

Source: ADB Project Team.

In the countryside, the food items distributed were sufficient; however, in urban areas, the amount was reported to be insufficient, with these areas needing additional support. Following an assessment, local levels provided more to needy people and families, notably in the urban areas. Some local levels coordinated with the private sector in the urban areas to mobilize cooked food and noncooked food items from the food bank. By distributing food in a timely manner to needy people, the local levels could, to some extent, protect the vulnerable groups from falling into the trap of high-interest loans and thus long-term financial crisis.

Public works programs (such as the cash-for-work program of the Ministry of Labor, Employment, and Social Security, and the Prime Minister Employment Program) and other donors helped address food insecurity, underemployment, and chronic poverty among the working-age population. These programs can be considered an alternative means of addressing such issues during crisis, including involving or motivating local levels to offer similar activities locally through employment dialogue forums. Box 1 summarizes the alternative approach taken by Rambha Rural Municipality.

Gender and Inclusion: Specific Needs, Capacities, and Interests in Food Distribution

During the lockdown, it was challenging to address issues related to unorganized occupational groups and, particularly, vulnerable women—that is, pregnant and lactating mothers. A key role of the local levels is to ensure better protection and health for these groups (as well as for their children) and, at the same time, to encourage local partners to provide specific support. The study explored (i) the extent to which the local levels were successful in identifying and addressing the specific needs of people in this category, (ii) the support that local levels provided, and (iii) local level engagement in bringing out innovative ideas and activities to address the issues.

BOX 1: From Food Relief to Employment Generation

From 4 April 2020, Rambha Rural Municipality began distributing food relief to vulnerable people in all five of its wards. On 25 April 2020, the local level delivered relief for the second time. The food distribution program benefited a total of 1,093 people. People continued to demand food assistance to answer their daily needs. The local level then switched to creating job opportunities for needy people, while following health protocols. Chair of Rambha Rural Municipality (Bishnu Prasad Bhandari) said, "We considered that providing employment opportunities while maintaining health protocols was a better option than food relief; thus, we initiated cash-for-work projects."

Two such projects were implemented during the last month of fiscal year 2020 (July). The Bakumphedi Trail Improvement Project provided employment to 40 people (25 females and 15 males, all from a disadvantaged group community), and the Badarkhola Mathillo Ghyangsing Road Upgrading Project employed 40 people (36 from a disadvantaged group and 4 from another group). Employed people were paid NRs460 per day. The cash-for-work program generated 880 person-days of employment during the lockdown period.

Similarly, Ward 6 of Manahari Rural Municipality adopted a cash-for-work approach to meet the food demands of vulnerable people. The chair of the ward reported that they shifted to cash-for-work in ward-level projects after distributing food relief to 381 households.

Source: ADB Project Team.

Specific Needs Addressed

Almost all sampled local levels initially identified the needs of women, pregnant and lactating mothers, PWDs, and the marginalized communities, including migrant workers, and provided support accordingly. In addition to specific food support, the local levels provided transportation support to individuals, including a free ambulance service for PWDs and women who had recently given birth, etc. Table 7 shows the specific needs that local levels addressed for pregnant women, lactating mothers, PWDs, and the marginalized communities.

Identifying people with specific needs from unorganized occupational groups, including migrant laborers, and providing support accordingly were both difficult tasks. Local levels had no formal profile of such people. However, local levels demonstrated good practice in addressing protection issues and in providing nutritious food (e.g., milk, ghee, Horlicks, meat, eggs, fruits, and vegetables) for pregnant and lactating women, PWDs, and single women, considering local practices.

In addition to nutritious food support, local levels provided sanitary kits, including slippers, clothes, etc., and free transportation for PWDs as necessary. Awareness of different gender and inclusion-specific risks and vulnerabilities was common in the local levels, which were capable of addressing these while distributing food.

Table 7: Specific Needs Addressed for Pregnant Women, Lactating Mothers, People with Disabilities, and the Marginalized Communities

Local Level	Needs Identified Yes	Needs Identified No	Support Provided
Bideha	✓		Mayor randomly distributing nutritious food (soybeans, chickpeas, sugar) to pregnant women at his discretion
Birendranagar	✓		Targeted food support to 27 people with disabilities; targeted food support to 54 single women (widowed, divorced, or separated); *sutkeri* (post-birth mother) packs, with door-to-door service; nutritious food for newborns, with door-to-door service
Dhangadi	✓		Through nongovernment organizations; local level not involved directly
Manahari		✓	No activity at community level in terms of specific support
Pokhara	✓		NRs500 to mothers within 60 days of giving birth for their own food nourishment; dialysis for patients and *sutkeris* provided with free ambulance services; nutrition package (equivalent to NRs2,000) to 1,400 *sutkeris* during lockdown
Rambha	✓		Eggs for pregnant and lactating women and nutritious baby food (Lito) for children aged 6–24 months, with the support of the Chief Minister's Rural Development Program during the lockdown
Rangeli	✓		Additional foodstuffs (same food as distributed to others) to family; nutritious food, such as 0.5 kg ghee and Horlicks, to each pregnant women with 2-month interval
Suddodhan	✓		Horlicks, Chewanpras, 15 eggs, and 0.5 kg ghee provided to elderly people and beneficiaries of the Golden 1,000 Days; TDOs took data from female community health volunteers of respective settlement/ward and coordinated with the ward office for distribution

kg = kilogram, NRs = Nepalese rupees, TDO = tole development organization.

Source: ADB Project Team.

Involvement of Organizations and Individuals in Specific Support

Five local levels out of nine coordinated with NGOs and CBOs to provide specific support to needy people through the local level's "single door" policy. In Bideha, Aasaman Nepal provided nutritious food (soybeans, chickpeas, sugar) to pregnant women. In Manahari, health facilities provided delivery allowance to mothers post-birth, the Red Cross gave sanitary kits to those in home quarantine, and ActionAid Nepal provided food packages to 148 female beneficiaries. NGOs in Suddodhan provided specific support to 303 women under the Golden 1,000 Days. Local levels provided nutritious food (Poshan Jhola) to marginalized women with support (NRs 350,000) from the provincial government. Similarly, NGOs in Birendranagar provided food support to PWDs, newborns, and single women. Mercy Corps and a few other organizations in Dhangadi distributed foodstuffs and other materials to address the specific needs of children and women.

Addressing Specific Needs in Quarantine

The specific needs of women, PWDs, and marginalized people in quarantine were addressed. Except in the case of Birendranagar, most of the sampled local levels offered the needed assistance. In addition to food packages, local levels also distributed sanitary kits and other water, sanitation, and hygiene-related materials. Box 2 presents the case of a pregnant woman from Rambha 2 receiving local-level support while in quarantine. Meanwhile, Table 8 summarizes the specific support given by sampled local levels during quarantine.

Addressing Issues Related to People with Disabilities

According to responses from selected local levels, PWDs were the hardest hit during the lockdown period given their functional limitations and environmental barriers. Local levels followed different approaches in addressing their needs (Table 9). Respondents clearly indicated that food items were in the highest demand, followed by health and hygiene materials.

BOX 2: Specific Food Support in an Isolation Center

Ramisara Hiski, a 23-year-old woman from Rambha 2, Phoksingkot, works in India with her husband as a migrant laborer. Pregnant and with a daughter of 18 months, she arrived in her hometown from India with her husband on 12 June 2020. They were quarantined in Sanahungi Secondary School. Her husband and daughter both tested positive for COVID-19. Although Ramisara was not infected, she had to stay in the isolation center to take care of her child. The primary health center located nearby provided health services for people in the isolation center. On 6 July 2020, Ramisara gave birth to a baby boy in the isolation center. A medical officer and two nurses from the primary health center provided appropriate neonatal and maternal health services. The local level also provided ghee, meat, eggs, and milk to the isolation center so she could meet her health and dietary needs. Radha Kumari Shrestha, vice-chair of Rambha Rural Municipality, assigned as coordinator of the isolation center, said, "As a woman, I was aware of her specific needs in terms of food and logistics at the time, so I guided the isolation center staff to provide nutritious foods such as ghee, meat, eggs, and fruits as recommended by the health personnel. In addition, for a couple of days, I myself cooked local chicken, rice with ghee, and hot soup at home and provided it to her." On 10 July, Ramisara was discharged for home quarantine with her family members. As per government rulings, she was also given a transportation allowance of NRs2,000. Ramisara expressed her view with regard to the support she had received from the local level: "If I had been on the way traveling or at home at the time of delivery, my health would have been at risk. During my stay at the isolation center, I received adequate medical treatment and nutritious meals."

Source: ADB Project Team.

Table 8: Addressing Specific Needs in Quarantine

| Local Level | Needs Identified | | Support Provided |
	Yes	No	
Bideha	✓		Hygienic cooked food, mosquito nets, slippers
Birendranagar		✓	Common food for all women
Manahari	✓		Nutritious food (meat and eggs) for pregnant and lactating women; sanitary kits
Pokhara	✓		Food for others; sanitary kits for women
Rambha	✓		Food for others; specific food for the needy under guidance of the vice-chair of Rambha Rural Municipality
Rangeli	✓		Nutritious food, such as 0.5 kg ghee and Horlicks, for pregnant women; provision for caretakers to stay in quarantine to take care of child; fruit from time to time; sanitary pads for women
Suddodhan	✓		Money provided to concerned households for food; family members responsible for carrying food from home to quarantine; amount per family differs as per local level decision on the basis of local prices

kg = kilogram.

Source: Asian Development Bank project team.

Table 9: Specific Support Provided to People with Disabilities

Local Level	Specific Support Provided during Lockdown
Bideha	Food provided at home.
Birendranagar	Food provided to PWDs based on demand on doorstep.
Dhangadi	PWDs provided with kit bags and COVID-19 safety materials.
Manahari	Foodstuff provided on doorstep.
Pokhara	PWD umbrella organization, Netrahin Sangh, advocated with the municipal office for relief materials for blind people; this was addressed accordingly. According to respondents from the organization, service providers did not proactively identify the specific needs of PWDs; however, PWDs were supported with foodstuff two or three times.
Rambha	Foodstuff delivered to people who could not come to fetch their food package from the distribution center (about 60 out of 338 households).
Rangeli	Foodstuff provided on doorstep, clothes to individuals, and sanitary pads for women.
Suddodhan	Wheelchairs distributed to PWDs.

COVID-19 = coronavirus disease, PWD = person with disability.

Source: ADB Project Team.

Risks and Vulnerabilities in Food Distribution

Key Risks Associated with Food Distribution and Mitigation Measures

Key risks associated with food distribution were identified as follows: (i) limited access to the market or distribution centers, (ii) difficulties maintaining COVID-19 protocols during distribution, (iii) the obligation to produce personal identification, (iv) issues related to food sufficiency and timely delivery, and (v) selection criteria not being strictly followed. Beneficiaries had grievances related to political party and/or elected representatives favoring their voters in supporting food relief to vulnerable people. Respondents in Ward 7 of Rangeli Municipality said they had faced demand for foodstuffs from fake households from the same family, which sometimes created complications during distribution. Respondents in Dhangadi stated that the local level initially did not prepare common parameters for selecting real beneficiaries to provide to the ward offices. Ward offices were responsible for selecting beneficiaries using their own judgment. However, ward offices and the respective relief committees later prepared a database of beneficiaries and the municipality dealt with some of the left-out beneficiaries. The majority of focus group discussion (FGD) respondents highlighted that the quantity of food relief distributed within the community was insufficient and that food was not provided in time. Limited preparedness meant that data availability on needy people remained an issue.

Respondents from Bideha Municipality minimized these issues by mobilizing local political leaders to select beneficiaries and distribute food to the needy. According to respondents in Rambha Municipality, both providers and receivers followed health protocols while distributing and receiving foodstuffs. Food distributors prepared the packages of food items based on family size and kept them in a row; the poor and vulnerable people came and picked up their packs while maintaining social distancing. Food distributors also provided food for people obtaining social security allowances, as these people had not received their allowances for the past 4 months. Homnath Gaire, Nepal Urban Resilience Project staff and a member of the Food Support Study Team in Pokhara, highlighted that the local level had also provided food relief to temporary foreign citizen residents in Pokhara Metropolitan City.[8] Ward-level respondents in Birendranagar Municipality indicated that there was minimum risk involved in the distribution process in their respective wards, but the COVID-19 protocol was nevertheless followed. Respondents in Rambha Rural Municipality mentioned that they had even provided food assistance to people without official identification.

Different Impacts of Lockdown and Food Shortage on Women, Men, Disadvantaged Groups, and People with Disabilities

Respondents highlighted the impossibility of fulfilling daily family needs as a result of loss of daily wages, which further aggravated their frustration and anxiety.[9] The major observations made by stakeholders in interviews were as follows: (i) incidence of mental health issues and gender-based violence (GBV) increased; (ii) health checkups, such as antenatal care and postnatal care visits at health facilities, were irregular; (iii) education of children became sporadic; (iv) women and children in transit districts were highly affected because of lack of nutritious food; and (v) vegetables and fruits were wasted because of the shutdown of markets, resulting in them not distributed to needy people locally. Ward-level respondents in Suddodhan Rural Municipality said that the pandemic situation significantly raised awareness on personal health and hygiene at the community level despite its several adverse impacts, which included economic crisis, obstruction to regular education, and discontinued employment.

Punam Sapkota, social worker in Rangeli Municipality, reported that mobility restrictions affected antenatal care and postnatal care visits. She added that both male and female household members experienced

---

[8] Pokhara Metropolitan City conducted a rapid assessment on the food distribution program by forming a 13-member study team.
[9] Respondents include beneficiaries and representatives of the media, NGOs, and municipalities.

mental stress as a result of the economic crisis. The local women's network coordinated and collaborated with the municipality to provide nutritious food items to pregnant and lactating women. Respondents from the District Red Cross in Surkhet said that orphans, people from other districts working in Surkhet for a daily wage, and migrants from India and other districts in transit in Surkhet were highly affected. The District Red Cross, with the support of the United Nations Children's Fund (UNICEF), managed cooked food, safer stays, and transportation. As reported by female respondents in Dhangadi 11, male family members stayed at home as they lost employment opportunities. GBV accelerated. Vegetables were wasted in the field because of the closure of the transport distribution network. The food crisis was exacerbated among families that were already facing food insecurity even before the pandemic. Participants also highlighted the risks of different nutritional and mental health issues among vulnerable populations.

Maintaining Self-Esteem for Poor and Vulnerable Groups

Support to meet basic needs in emergency and crisis is a fundamental right of every citizen, including poor and vulnerable groups.. Groups including orphans, the elderly, single women with children, PWDs, people living with HIV, patients with tuberculosis and other chronic illnesses, etc., need special protection and care during pandemics. In most cases of food distribution, local levels do not seem to have taken sufficient care while publicizing beneficiaries' plight, and even did not seek the beneficiaries' consent while taking pictures and displaying them (Box 3). Local levels and local food supporters used these techniques to discourage well-off people or families from trying to grab free food for themselves. Many respondents pointed to the fact that the self-esteem and rights of vulnerable people should have been safeguarded while distributing food relief.

Health and Sanitation

Local levels faced a major challenge in maintaining health and sanitation facilities in quarantine and isolation centers. Local levels highlighted their efforts in creating awareness, providing health and sanitation

support in quarantine, and serving fresh food from in-house kitchens, hotels, and, in some cases, beneficiaries' own houses. Local levels managed safe drinking water and toilet facilities within the premises of quarantine and isolation centers, providing both temporary and permanent supplies of drinking water and sanitation. During this period, local levels added some permanent water supply and sanitation facilities in health posts and schools where quarantine and isolation facilities were extended.

Respondents in Dhangadi confirmed that food was managed at three levels according to the local context: from hotels to beneficiaries, from supporting organizations, and from beneficiary's family. Drinking water, sanitation, and health facilities were well facilitated in quarantine centers. Beneficiaries were provided with sanitizer, soap, and other sanitation items. However, media representatives had a different view, particularly stating that water and sanitation facilities were not properly maintained and there were insufficient toilets and drinking water facilities.

> ### BOX 3: Self-Esteem and the Rights of Beneficiaries
>
> Local levels followed different practices to minimize the misuse of free foodstuffs during the lockdown period. Providing cooked food to needy people in city areas, taking photos of beneficiaries receiving foodstuffs, and having receivers sign declarations of income were the key practices. Moti Bahadur Thapa, an Informal Sector Service Center official in Suddodhan Rural Municipality, claimed that, while taking photos of foodstuffs being delivered and sharing them on social media may have reduced the huge demand from well-off families and helped poor people, distributors should have respected the self-esteem and human rights of individuals. He further said that he had met some poor people who would prefer to borrow groceries rather than being photographed for receiving food relief.
>
> Source: ADB Project Team.

Respondents from Bideha Municipality reported separate rooms and toilets for females; mineral water provided to beneficiaries; and female community health volunteers (FCHVs), auxiliary nurse, midwives, and staff nurses deployed for service to needy women. Respondents in Manahari said that the local level provided sanitary kits (slippers, combs, toothpaste, brushes, soap, etc.). Similarly, respondents from Rangeli mentioned that the local level had addressed the specific health requirements of the elderly, pregnant women, and children. Overall, most local levels highlighted that they were well aware of issues related to hygienic food, health, and sanitation, and support was provided to beneficiaries in quarantine and in communities.

The effects of the crisis on children of the poor and vulnerable households were severe, resulting in less nutritious food and deferred health treatment. The study could not guarantee that local levels had made significant efforts to support children in terms of providing nutritious food and quality health-care services. Because of the priority given to COVID-19 issues in health care, children suffered and were even deprived of normal care during the period of the extreme spread of COVID-19 cases. The regular allotment of nutritious food to children, including antenatal care and postnatal care visits, was disturbed.

Women's Participation and Decision-Making Opportunities

Local levels reported that they had formed COVID-19 coordination committees at the municipal and ward levels, with participation from political party representatives, NGOs and CBOs, social workers, security personnel, the media, and Red Cross representative. Committee activities included regularly conducting meetings to discuss and manage the food response, maintaining the minutes of meetings, selecting beneficiaries, and monitoring food distribution. In all activities, women's participation and decision-making opportunities were ensured.

The participation level of women in decision-making for beneficiary selection and food distribution was satisfactory, although it varied from one local level to another (Table 10). However, participation of women

at community level was token in most cases, though great passion was still observed among women in the decision-making and management of food distribution. The participation of vulnerable people and PWDs was limited in almost all the local levels, owing to the risk of COVID-19 infection and mobility restrictions.

Most respondents mentioned difficulties, especially for women, in overcoming mobility restrictions imposed not only by the government but also by family members. Most women were busy with household chores such as kitchen work and looking after the children and older people. As discussed with respondents in Rambha Rural Municipality, the constraints to women's participation in decision-making were traditional practices (staying at home), low confidence of girls and women, and low levels of encouragement by family counterparts. Similarly, respondents in Rangeli and Dhangadi mentioned that women and people from vulnerable groups generally are not involved in social work because of low levels of awareness, low confidence, and other cultural as well as religious factors.

Key informant interview (KII) respondents in Dhangadi Submetropolitan City stated that the key element in women's participation to the process was their dedication to social work. KII respondents in Birendranagar highlighted the usefulness of the participation of women and beneficiaries in resolving grievances. Women members of the quarantine management committee played a mediating role whenever there was a disagreement between men and women in the quarantine center.

Rights and Gender-Based Violence during Lockdown

Primary Reasons for Gender-Based Violence during Lockdown

The COVID-19 pandemic caused widespread job losses, resulting in economic strain on vulnerable people, especially for those working in the informal sector. Respondents of municipalities reported an increase in domestic violence and GBV cases, primarily because of an increased trend of returning migrant workers, job losses and lack of alternative income

Table 10: Women's Participation in the Selection of Beneficiaries and the Distribution of Food

Local Level/ Ward	Distribution Structure	Number and % of Women	Women Representation	Respondent Satisfaction (1=Worst, 5=Best)
Bideha, Ward 5	12 members from all-party committee	3 (25%)	Elected representatives, FCHVs	2
Birendranagar, Ward 6	Loose committee of 16 members formed from ward and TDOs	8 (50%)	Elected representatives, TDO members, municipal staff, teachers	3
Dhangadi, Ward 11	Loose committee of 7 members led by ward chair	4 (57%)	Social workers, municipal staff, elected representatives, FCHVs	3
Manahari, Ward 6	Facilitated by 11-member all-party committee	5 (45%)	Teachers, FCHVs, women elected representatives	3
Pokhara, Ward 5	Facilitated by 31-member committee	8 (26%)	Social workers/TDO members, municipal staff, elected representatives	2
Rambha, Ward 1	Committee of 8 people under ward chair with all-party representatives and health and police staff	3 (38%)	Elected representatives, health personnel	2
Rangeli, Ward 7	Political representatives' committee of 7 people	3 (43%)	Social workers, municipal staff, FCHVs, teachers, elected representatives	3
Suddodhan, Ward 4	Loose committee of 7 people formed by TDOs and mothers' groups led by ward chair	4 (57%)	TDO members, members from mothers' groups	3

FCHV = female community health volunteer, TDO = tole development organization.

Source: ADB Project Team.

sources, home confinement for an uncertain period of time, and food insufficiency and nonavailability of choice food. With limited income sources, male frustration was taken out on female members of the family. Beneficiaries of food support in Dhangadi 11 said that the key reason for domestic violence and GBV was decreased income. Male family members were also asking money for alcohol from their partners. However, the chair of Ward 5 in Bideha expressed that alcohol shops were totally closed during the lockdown and cases of domestic violence and GBV in the area decreased as a result of the reduction in alcohol consumption by male family members.

Activities Conducted by the Local Levels to Reduce the Incidence of Violence

Despite limited resources and other priorities in addressing the COVID-19 pandemic situation, local levels and local organizations took steps to deliver support to GBV survivors. Initiatives included activation of local-level judicial committees, mobilization of trained mediators, counseling via telephone, intermediation and counseling by local elected representatives, and awareness-raising activities through local media and social networks. Respondents of Dhangadi said that the deputy mayor handled cases directly throughout the lockdown with the help of ward-level representatives, trained mediators, and counselors. This was in spite of having multiple responsibilities, such as revenue estimation, planning and budgeting, monitoring and evaluation, and NGO coordination. Sometimes, deputy mayors were not clear on their judicial role. The deputy mayor of Dhangadi handled cases via virtual means such as Messenger and WhatsApp calls, mobile calls, and discussions with parties concerned. Respondents in Pokhara Metropolitan City reported that the Municipal Judicial Committee offered online and telephone services for domestic violence and GBV case registration (three cases were found to have been registered).

During lockdown, district courts were closed. However, the majority of local level respondents reported that legal service providers and courts should have an emergency service even during pandemic and disaster situations. Although deputy mayors and vice-chairs were not conversant with legal provisions, judiciary committees tried their best to mediate cases with limited referral to legal entities. The major role of the committees was to facilitate safe home services, legal services, and health services, as well as to handle domestic violence and GBV referral cases. "Cases definitely increased compared with normal circumstances, and it was obviously difficult to handle the cases, but we mobilized the network developed at the local level," said Punam Sapkota, a social worker in Rangeli Municipality.

KII, small group interview (SGI), and FGD respondents all said that domestic violence incidence was on the rise during the lockdown. Respondents further mentioned that local levels did not respond to domestic violence cases promptly because they preferred to respond to COVID-19 issues and manage COVID-19 referral cases. Meanwhile, judiciary committees could not provide adequate services because local levels remained closed during the lockdown. Respondents from Rambha Rural Municipality stated that no cases were registered in the municipal and ward offices. However, respondents reported that unregistered domestic violence cases were settled in the presence of elected representatives and police. Respondents from the Red Cross in Rupandehi District (where Rambha Rural Municipality is situated said that local

levels mobilized psychosocial counselors and elected representatives to settle cases through either in-person or virtual means. Similarly, they provided training and orientation to elected representatives, staff of local levels, and mediators on domestic violence and GBV during pandemic situations.

Most respondents showed concern about protecting women and girls from violence during the pandemic and lockdown. However, getting actual data on cases was a major challenge at the local level. The survivors themselves resisted reporting to the concerned authorities because of a culture of silence and fear. With cases on a rising trend prior to COVID-19, the situation demanded more attention during the pandemic. This is a wake-up call to the local levels and other relevant stakeholders and individuals, encouraging them to pay attention and take action to prevent cases of domestic violence and GBV during pandemics and disasters.

Resource Management

Budget Leveraged from Different Sources

The COVID-19 Prevention, Control, and Treatment Fund of the Government of Nepal became operational following a guideline approved by the Council of Ministers on 22 March 2020. The Financial Comptroller General Office operationalized the fund at the federal level by establishing the Fund Operation Committee, which was responsible for disbursement of the fund to the local levels, provincial governments, and other line agencies. Following this procedure adopted by the federal government, provincial governments and local levels established and operationalized the COVID-19 funds.

Managing resources, including identifying sources of funds to procure food relief items, was a bigger challenge for the local levels as the demand for food relief continued to rise during the lockdown. Respondents were asked about contributions made by the private sector and international and national NGOs in supporting budget and other food items for the relief work. During the discussion, the study team observed that the main sources of budget were the internal resources of the local levels; the federal government; the provincial government; and the private sector, NGOs, and individuals. Three out of the nine local levels (Dhangadi, Rambha, and Suddodhan) received a budget from the federal government in their COVID-19 fund. However, all local levels were provided with support from the provincial government.

All local levels formally asked the private sector, NGOs, individuals, and civil society to provide resources through their COVID-19 fund. Out of the nine local levels, eight received cash support from the private sector, NGOs, and individuals. The amount of support varied among local levels based on the willingness of the resource granters and the initiation and coordination of the local level. Respondents from Pokhara Metropolitan City reported the highest amount (approximately NRs6.5 million), whereas Manahari collected around NRs100,000 only. As highlighted by KII respondents, some local levels (Pokhara, Rambha, and Suddodhan) collected cash from municipal staff and elected representatives as well. In addition, some local levels (Rangeli and Suddodhan) collected in-kind resources (food items) from the private sector, such as individuals, businesspeople, industrialists, NGOs, CBOs, etc.

Box 4 shows the exemplary practice of Suddodhan Rural Municipality in collecting resources (such as cash, in-kind support, and food items) from external sources. Suddodhan collected approximately one-third of the COVID-19 fund from the private sector, cooperatives, and individuals.

The major challenges facing local levels in mobilizing the necessary resources related to transferring development budget allocations, soliciting donations from the private sector, and managing local levels' own limited disaster funds. Most local levels (except Pokhara) reported that they had transferred the development budget to the COVID-19 relief fund as the demand for foodstuffs was high and they

BOX 4: Mobilization of the Private Sector for Resource Generation

Suddodhan Rural Municipality collected significant support (both in cash and in kind) for food relief from the local private sector to assist vulnerable people during the lockdown. Industrialists, businesspeople, cooperatives, villagers, and others provided cash and foodstuff amounting to NRs2,016,736. As the local level spent NRs2,406,736 on overall food relief, local contributions accounted for 83.8% of the expense. Rajendra Kadel, chair of Ward 4, reported that the local level and the tole development organizations worked together in a very efficient manner to collect cash and in-kind support from the private sector and distributed them to the needy people in the community and those in quarantine or in isolation. The ward office established a relief collection center with a management committee involving all political parties, local cooperatives, and tole development organizations responsible for distribution. The committee gained the confidence of all the private sector donors and also collected significant support from the nongovernment sector.

Source: ADB Project Team.

had insufficient resources. The audit report of the Office of the Auditor General for FY 2020 revealed that both Janakpurdham and Rangeli local levels transferred NRs20 million from other budget heads to their COVID-19 funds. Some local levels (Bideha and Manahari) reported that they could not generate significant resources from the private sector despite their efforts. Table 11 shows the COVID-19 budget sources of the nine sampled local levels.

Table 11: Resources for the Pandemic Response including Food Relief Distribution

| Local Level | Budget Source (NRs) | | | | Total Budget/ Resources |
	Federal Government	Provincial Government	Local Level Internal Resources	Others (Private Sector/ NGOs)	
Bideha	0	1,500,000	10,432,000	0	11,932,000
Birendranagar	0	3,000,000	68,865,533	1,028,467	72,894,000
Dhangadi	9,680,175	6,270,000	21,562,475	641,811	38,154,461
Janakpurdham	0	2,000,000	31,346,314	572,010	33,918,324
Manahari	0	1,000,000	8,300,000	100,000	9,400,000
Pokhara	0	10,000,000	59,542,975	6,478,770	76,021,745
Rambha	256,000	1,000,000	7,400,000	2,604,432	11,260,432
Rangeli	0	6,000,000	16,374,537	384,963	22,759,500
Suddodhan	1,390,000	1,000,000	2,000,000	2,016,737	6,406,737
Total	**11,326,175**	**31,770,000**	**225,823,834**	**13,827,190**	**282,747,199**
Share	**4.01%**	**11.24%**	**79.87%**	**4.89%**	**100.00%**

NGO = nongovernment organization, NRs = Nepalese rupees.

Note: Percentages may not total 100% because of rounding.

Sources: Audit Report of the Office of the Auditor General for Fiscal Year 2020, and the Crisis Management Information System.

Figure 1: Budget Sources for the Pandemic Response by Share

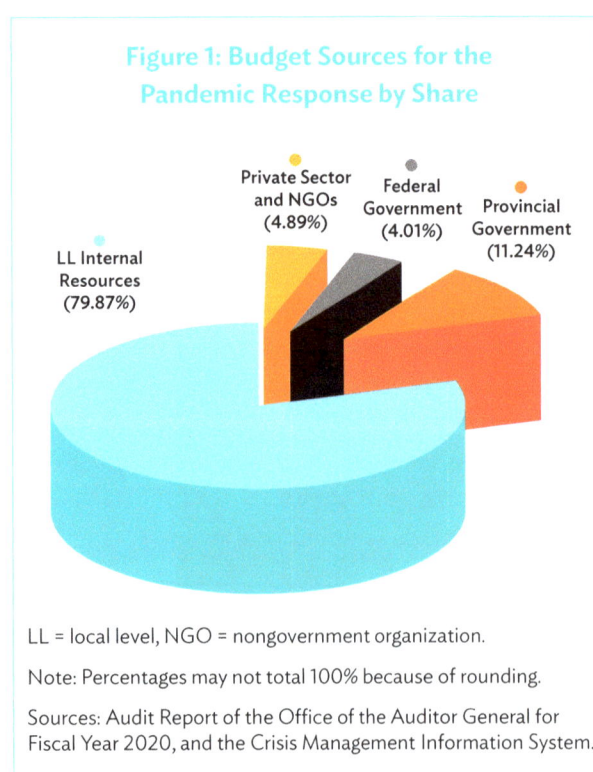

Private Sector and NGOs (4.89%)
Federal Government (4.01%)
Provincial Government (11.24%)
LL Internal Resources (79.87%)

LL = local level, NGO = nongovernment organization.

Note: Percentages may not total 100% because of rounding.

Sources: Audit Report of the Office of the Auditor General for Fiscal Year 2020, and the Crisis Management Information System.

In total, nine local levels managed NRs282.7 million for their COVID-19 relief work. As shown in Figure 1, local levels' own resources constituted the highest proportion, at 79.87%, followed by support from the provincial government (11.24%). Interestingly, support from the private sector, NGOs, cooperatives, municipal staff and elected representatives, and civil society (4.89%) exceeded the grant from the federal government (4.01%).

Expenditure on Food Relief Distribution

The nine local levels reported that they had spent 37.16% of the total available resources in the COVID-19 fund on food relief, with Rambha spending the lowest share (8.05%) and Janakpurdham the highest (59.15%) (Table 12). In terms of amount spent on food distribution, Pokhara spent the highest (NRs31,669,000) and Rambha the lowest (NRs906,860). KII respondents from Suddodhan reported that the local level had satisfied food relief demand, mobilizing resources largely from the private sector.

Table 12: Details on the Mobilization of Funding for Food Relief Distribution

Local Level	Total Budget (NRs)	Food Expense Amount (NRs)	Food Expense Share
Bideha	11,932,000	3,551,400	29.76%
Birendra Nagar	72,894,000	22,688,325	31.13%
Dhangadi	38,154,461	9,319,987	24.43%
Janakpurdham	33,918,324	20,064,204	59.15%
Manahari	9,400,000	5,041,709	53.64%
Pokhara	76,021,745	31,669,000	41.66%
Rambha	11,260,432	906,860	8.05%
Rangeli	22,759,500	10,552,912	46.37%
Suddodhan	6,406,737	1,266,723	19.77%
Total	**282,747,199**	**105,061,120**	**37.16%**

NRs = Nepalese rupees.

Sources: Audit Report of the Office of the Auditor General for Fiscal Year 2020, and the Crisis Management Information System.

Procurement of Goods and Quality of Food

Procurement of Food Items

The study assessed the food procurement processes adopted by the local levels during the lockdown period. Most local levels reported adopting a direct purchase method, claiming that the prices paid for the food items were competitive. For instance, the mayor of Bideha said, "We mobilized members of the municipal-level COVID-19 management committee, representing political parties, to identify suppliers who could provide food items at lower prices for procuring under direct purchase." Only three local levels (Birendranagar, Dhangadi, and Janakpurdham) adopted a sealed quotation method to procure food items. Manahari reported some constraints in purchasing food items during the lockdown period owing to the reluctance of shops to open, low food supplies, price hikes, and unknown quantities of food stock at the local level. Manahari further clarified that a direct method of purchasing was adopted to enable a quick response to demand for food from vulnerable people. Rangeli respondents said that they had purchased and stored sufficient food from the local rice mill amid speculation regarding food shortages during lockdowns.

The responsibility for purchasing food was shared differently in different local levels. The study team observed that (i) Rangeli did not assign anyone to purchase food and the mayor led the procurement process; (ii) Manahari, Pokhara, and Rambha mobilized respective ward offices and reimbursed the cost later; (iii) Bideha, Dhangadi, and Janakpurdham assigned the chief administrative officer, including municipal staff, to purchase food items; (iv) Suddodhan assigned the respective ward-level all-party committee and quarantine management committee to purchase food items together; and (v) Birendranagar assigned the procurement unit of the local level to purchase food items. The senior officer of Janakpurdham, Ganesh Prasad Yadav, mentioned that procurement was not carried out through the ward level because of inadequate capacity at that level; finding the goods at one cost center was efficient and less time-consuming.

Most local levels purchased food from local private shops and suppliers, while some used government-owned entities like the Food Management and Trading Company and the Salt Trading Corporation (Figure 2). Bideha purchased oil, soap, and sugar from the Salt Trading Corporation and other food items from private suppliers. Similarly, Birendranagar purchased food from the depot of the Food Management and Trading Company and the Salt Trading Corporation when they had stocks. Respondents of Ward 6 of Birendranagar said that food was initially purchased from the Nepal depot of the Food Management and Trading Company but, after complaints were received on the quality, further purchasing was made from private food suppliers at the same negotiated price. This response indicates that the quality of food supplied from government-owned entities was not fully reliable. Exceptionally, Suddodhan purchased food from a local cooperative shop, with respondents claiming they had purchased it at a lower-than-market price. Janakpurdham purchased rice from Biratnagar (around 200 kilometers away) as the supplier got the contract through a bidding competition.

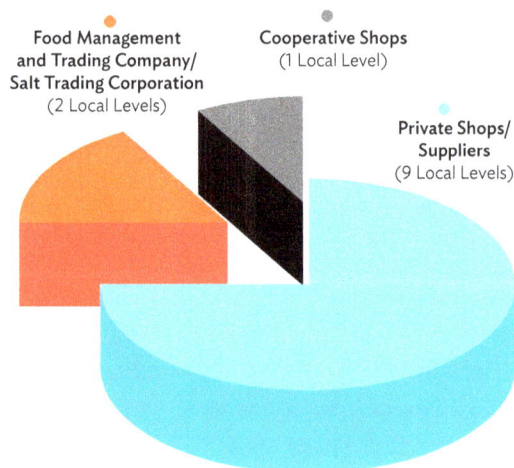

Figure 2: Sources of Purchased Food Items, Multiple Responses

Food Management and Trading Company/ Salt Trading Corporation (2 Local Levels)

Cooperative Shops (1 Local Level)

Private Shops/ Suppliers (9 Local Levels)

Source: ADB Project Team.

Quality Assurance of Distributed Foods

The study team analyzed the monitoring of food quality before dispatch to distribution centers or people. Overall, this was carried out by municipal or ward staff and elected representatives, including party representatives associated with the respective local level.

Respondents from Manahari, Pokhara, Rambha, and Suddodhan reported that ward staff and elected representatives monitored food quality and quantity. In Bideha, Birendranagar, Dhangadi, Janakpurdham, and Rangeli, food (quality and quantity) was monitored by municipal staff and elected representatives before it was dispatched to ward and/or distribution centers. Bideha monitored food quality before food items were packaged in the local level premises where they were stored. Respondents from Birendranagar reported that only general observations were made in evaluating the quality of food items, given the nonavailability of technical expertise to test them. Encouragingly, Janakpurdham tested food quality (rice and oil) through officials of the Food Technology and Quality Control Office, Janakpur, before distribution (Box 5). Dhangadi claimed that the quality was monitored by sampling before dispatch to ward offices. Beneficiaries of Ward 11 reported that 25 packs of damaged rice were discovered and returned to the municipality. An Informal Sector Service Center representative of Suddodhan, Moti Bahadur Thapa, reported that, "The ward committee monitored the quality of food with the involvement of NGO and civil society."

On a scale of 1 to 5 (1 being the worst and 5 the best), respondents were asked to rate the quality and acceptability of the food delivered. Eight out of the nine sampled local levels (including ward respondents) rated the food distributed at 4 out of 5. Their rating was verified by third-party respondents (the private sector, NGO representatives, the media, social workers), except in Dhangadi, where a reporter from onlinekhabar.com rated the quality at 3 out of 5. Exceptionally, respondents from Suddodhan rated the quality at 5, which was later verified by the Informal Sector Service Center representative. The study found that the quality of food was better where civil society participation in distribution and monitoring was ensured.

Monitoring and Feedback Mechanism

Monitoring of the Food Distribution Process

Approaches to the monitoring of the food relief distribution, assessed during the study, varied from one local level to another. Bideha, Dhangadi, Janakpurdham, Rambha, and Rangeli reported that the quality and quantity of relief materials were monitored by elected representatives and municipal or ward staff. Rambha reported the involvement of the media. In Manahari and Pokhara, municipal and ward-level COVID-19 control and management committees monitored the quality and quantity of food relief. In addition, Pokhara formed a separate 14-member committee to carry out a rapid assessment of food distribution.[10] The committee forwarded its recommendations for improvements in the delivery process. Suddodhan formed a food relief distribution committee consisting of elected officials and representatives of the police, institutions, public schools, mothers' groups, youth clubs, cooperatives, NGOs, and CBOs to monitor the quality and quantity of distributed food items. Birendranagar reported that this task was carried out by the existing monitoring committee of the local level led by the deputy mayor. The ward chair of Birendranagar 6 added, "The ward-level COVID-19 management committee was also involved in the monitoring of food distribution."

As reported by the local levels, monitoring methods included visits and observations of distribution centers and discussions with beneficiaries to seek their comments and suggestions on relief work. The study found that there was no third-party monitoring mechanism to monitor the food distribution process. An NGO representative of Janakpur, Bishnu Kunwar, said, "There were no third-party monitoring mechanisms, and those involved in distribution also were involved in monitoring the relief distribution activities."

Respondents were asked about the proper use of cash assistance provided in applicable cases. Only Janakpurdham, Pokhara, and Suddodhan had provided cash as relief assistance. Pokhara had provided cash in two cases, with support from external sources. Respondents in Pokhara 5 said that cash was given by individual donors amounting to NRs16,000, spent on daily food requirements. Janakpurdham gave NRs300 to each family to purchase vegetable items. Ganesh Prasad Yadav, senior officer of Janakpurdham, confirmed that the amount provided was indeed used for vegetables. The chair of the Rural Development Forum in Janakpurdham, Bishnu Kunwar, said that the local level had not adopted any mechanism to track the use of cash assistance provided to vulnerable families. Suddodhan also reported proper use of cash support provided to households whose family members died as a result of COVID-19 infection. The local level reported that one male beneficiary from Ward 4 had sold the food to buy alcohol. After offering family counseling, the local level provided additional food support to the offender's household.

---

[10]   The committee consists of staff of the municipality, the Nepal Urban Resilience Project, and the police.

Feedback Mechanism

Municipal and ward-level respondents, the media, NGO staff, Red Cross representatives, and social workers reported that the local levels had not yet developed formal mechanisms for registering complaints and grievances, systems for the proper resolution of grievances, and feedback or reporting mechanisms. However, local levels had attempted to resolve verbal grievances received as far as possible. According to the local levels, grievances were related largely to eligibility of households for food relief support. One ward chair in Bideha reported that families that could afford their daily needs in lockdown nevertheless claimed food relief.

The chair of Rambha, Bishnu Prasad Bhandari, reported that there was no practice of registering grievances at the ward or municipal level; however, some families claiming to be eligible had made verbal complaints. The local level had considered these during the second selection process of families eligible for food relief. In Dhangadi, the ward office also reported verbal grievances regarding left-out households. These were provided with relief packages in the second phase. Encouragingly, Pokhara established a hotline service for the reporting of grievances, including other hardships raised as a result of mobility restrictions. The deputy mayor of Pokhara said that people had reported grievances regarding daily food requirements, which were addressed through the ward offices. The ward chair of Pokhara 5 said people reported grievances to elected representatives directly over the phone, and these were taken seriously and handled effectively. A different response was recorded in Rangeli. The local level provided food support to approximately 80% of households, so there were no grievances. In a third-party view, an NGO representative in Janakpurdham said that grievance mechanisms should be more accessible during crisis. During lockdown, mobility restrictions meant that there was limited ability to register grievances with the nearest government or local level.

Governance and Accountability

The study attempted to assess the governance and accountability of local levels in the food distribution process. This section discusses resource collection, information disclosure, public audit of expenditures, etc. As observed, local levels, through public notices, asked the private sector, NGOs, and individuals to support the COVID-19 fund for food relief and other humanitarian assistance to vulnerable people. All local levels reported that such support was disclosed through the website and/or notice board of the local level. Manahari reported that it had disclosed the name of the donor and the amount through the flex banner in the local level office. Similarly, Ward 5 of Pokhara published names and detail of support (cash and/or in kind) in the "Ward Darpan," a ward office publication.

Moreover, respondents were asked whether the local level had disclosed the ward-wise distributed quantity of food and expenditure on the ward notice board and website. Six local levels had disclosed expenditure on the website but not at the ward level. Among these, two local levels had disclosed details on quantity and expenditure on the municipal notice board. Manahari and Pokhara had disseminated ward-wise details of quantity distributed and expenditure. Dhangadi, Rambha, and Rangeli discussed expenditure and quantity of food in the municipal-level COVID-19 control and management committee and/or disaster management committee.

All of the local levels said that they had not conducted social or public audits on the expenditure of food support activities. Respondent from Suddodhan reported, "Given the risk of COVID-19 infection, a social or public audit of the expenditure incurred in food relief distribution was not conducted. However, expenditure was disclosed on the website of the local level." Birendranagar disseminated ward-wise expenditure at the TDO level and received feedback. During a public audit of the overall plan and projects of the local level, participants expressed their appreciation of the food relief's expenditure management.

As NGOs and CBOs are dependent on the local levels for their annual renewal of permission and consent to conduct their programming, their demand for a supporting role in local level activities is always overlooked. This is why NGOs and CBOs were not involved in ensuring accountability, according to Bishnu Kunwar, an NGO representative in Janakpurdham.

There was no feedback related to financial irregularities during food distribution from the media, social workers, NGO representatives, and beneficiaries. However, there was some feedback on food procurement in Dhangadi. A reporter from onlinekhabar.com said that a local newspaper had reported inedible food distributed in Ward 4. Further, a case is under investigation in the Commission for the Investigation of Abuse of Authority related to procurement of low-quality food.

Coordination and Mobilization of the Private Sector and Development Partners

Considering the need for timely resource mobilization and effective distribution of food relief, the local levels coordinated with stakeholders, including the federal and provincial governments, the private sector, and civil society. They adopted different practices to collect resources, mobilize human resources locally, and distribute through a single door system to keep grievances to a minimum. Resource management was challenging because there was a huge demand for

food relief during the lockdown period. The single door system helped in tracking resource mobilization and expenditure, maintaining safety and security, expediting beneficiary selection, and minimizing overlaps and gaps in distribution.

As the impact of the pandemic was unpredictable and the lockdown went on for a quite long time, the support of the private sector, development partners, and individuals was necessary to complement government efforts to provide food relief to vulnerable people. There were different practices in mobilizing support from nongovernment sectors, such as the food bank in Rupandehi Distict (Box 6). Rangeli adopted a single door policy to distribute food relief to vulnerable people. The local level also gave additional support to needy families by connecting them directly to the private sector and NGOs willing to distribute food relief. "During the mobilization of the private sector and NGOs, respective wards facilitated those donors in the distribution process to avoid duplication in food relief," the mayor of Rangeli said. Bideha formed all-party committees to collect food and relief materials from the private sector and development partners. However, the local level could not mobilize the nongovernment sector properly as collection from the private sector was nominal. The ward chair of Bideha 5 said, "In our ward, an NGO (Aasaman Nepal) distributed food relief to 10 ultra-poor households who already received food relief from the local level." Pokhara collected a significant amount (about NRs6.5 million) from the private sector, organizations, individuals, and municipal staff. To avoid

BOX 6: Food Bank in Rupandehi District for the Needy People

Food distribution from the federal and provincial governments across the country stopped after the initial distribution. However, in urban and industrial areas, there was considerable demand for food among unorganized occupational groups. Bhairahawa, Butwal, and Tillotamma local levels in Rupandehi collaborated with the local private sector, including tole development organizations, to assist vulnerable people as per demand. Industrialists, businesspeople, villagers, and others were asked to deposit foodstuffs voluntarily in a food bank. Kiran Malla, a senior officer of the Red Cross and a key informant interview respondent, stated that donors provided rice, pulses, salt, oil, and other items, as well as cash.

Source: ADB Project Team.

duplication, Pokhara instructed the private sector, individuals, and NGOs to obtain prior consent from the metropolitan office for distributing food relief.

Respondents from Manahari reported that they could not mobilize the private sector and NGOs significantly. They requested external support through a disaster management fund to be distributed through a single door system. Some religious institutions distributed food themselves without coordinating with the local level. A Red Cross representative from Manahari said that the initiative of the local level was not sufficient to mobilize external resources. Rambha issued a notice on the local radio and in newspapers seeking support for the COVID-19 fund. The local level adopted a single door policy for the collection and distribution of relief.

A different practice was observed in Suddodhan to mobilize resources from the private sector, NGOs, and individuals. A bank account was opened in the name of the chair of the local level and two ward chairs to collect cash and in-kind support. The local level mobilized about NRs2.0 million from municipal staff, individuals, NGOs, businesspeople, and industrialists, or around one-third of the total budget in the COVID-19 fund. Respondents from Dhangadi reported that the local level had a Mayor Welfare Fund to collect external resources. Meetings were conducted regularly, inviting the private sector and NGOs to donate resources. The local level adopted a single door policy to collect and mobilize resources from the nongovernment sector. However, the Madhesh and Sudurpaschi provincial governments also distributed food relief independently without coordinating with the respective local levels.

The private sector was more open than NGOs to providing relief support. NGOs supported food relief either from regular project activities or through immediate support from those working in the humanitarian field. A rapid survey on the role of social organizations and NGOs in the pandemic, conducted by the NGO Federation of Nepal, also revealed that organizations had contributed significantly to the response, including to food relief distribution.[11] Among 67 organizations from all provinces covered in the

study, 19 reported that they had provided food relief to laborers in the informal sector and 18 had provided food support to helpless people. Similarly, 14 organizations had provided nutritious food items and safety kits to people in home isolation. The report also mentions that receiving a travel pass from the government was the main challenge in working during the lockdown to support vulnerable people.

Disaster- and Pandemic-Responsive Planning at the Local Levels

Institutional and Legal Arrangements to Address Disasters and Pandemics

Each local level has a Disaster Risk Reduction and Management Act to respond to the impacts of disasters and pandemics. All sampled local levels had such an act as an institutional and legal arrangement for disaster preparedness, response, and victim rescue and rehabilitation. All local levels have formed a local-level disaster management committee as provisioned by the act. Overall, respondents reported that this committee performed effectively during the pandemic. Capacity constraints meant that disaster management committees at ward level were not functional in the COVID-19 response.

Although all local levels have disaster management funds to mitigate crisis impacts, these are insufficient. The chair of Rambha reported that the local level had had a practice of allocating NRs1.0 million to the disaster management fund in previous fiscal years. However, NRs3.0 million was allocated after the first surge of COVID-19. Bideha, Birendranagar, Janakpurdham, Manahari, and Pokhara have prepared a Disaster Fund Mobilization Guideline to facilitate the expenditure process through the disaster management fund. Birendranagar and Dhangadi have a Disaster Preparedness and Response Plan to reduce risk and manage the impacts of disasters. Respondents from Manahari and Pokhara said that the preparation of such a plan was in progress. Respondents from Rangeli highlighted that they had prepared a Flood Preparedness and Response Plan as part of lessons learned from

---

[11]   NGO Federation of Nepal. https://www.ngofederation.org/index.php/node/639.

frequent flooding. The food stock maintained at the municipality was handy for immediate distribution after the lockdown was imposed.

The Disaster Fund Mobilization Guidelines spell out expense provisions on relief materials, including food. The guideline of Pokhara mentions in para. 4(Ga) that one of the uses of the disaster management fund is to provide food relief to vulnerable people. Further to this, para. 8(7) mentions that if a family's housing, crops, land, or source of livelihood has been damaged as a result of disaster and they do not have anything to eat, they are to be provided with NRs10,000 per family as immediate relief for food. The guideline of Manahari also provisions the relief amount for disaster victims in its para. 22, for both partially affected and severely affected families. However, it does not specify the relief amount or support in terms of food.

Local-Level Capacity on Safety, Search, and Rescue

Local levels reportedly have some equipment for the search and rescue of victims of disaster.[12] All local levels reported that they coordinated with the Nepal Police and/or the Armed Police for immediate disaster response. Manahari and Rangeli provide search and rescue tools to police located within the local levels. Pokhara reported that the local level had tools. Municipalities in metropolitan and submetropolitan areas are better equipped than rural municipalities. However, they still do not have sufficient equipment to respond to disasters. Birendranagar Municipality reported, "We have some equipment but not sufficient, and no dedicated staff for disaster management and limited financial resources."

Rambha has limited equipment for search and rescue during a crisis. In the case of human resources, it has to rely on four police stations with limited equipment and a youth volunteer group of 27 members. Pokhara has 340 trained volunteers and 9 dedicated staff for an immediate response, and Manahari has 20 trained volunteers in each ward. Dhangadi has groups of trained volunteers with some tools.

Janakpurdham has established a Disaster Management and Emergency Service Center with necessary staff under the leadership of a section officer. This has various tools, including jackets, helmets, ropes, plastic buckets, picks, shovels, etc., as well as an ambulance and a fire brigade for emergency response. The section officer said that they had a volunteer group of 25 people for an immediate response. However, the local level does not have sufficient tools, including personal protective equipment. The local level further reported having limited human resources for the disaster management section; hence, the section officer is stretched to look after other activities besides disaster management.

Updating and Use of the Crisis Management Information System

With the outbreak of COVID-19, MOFAGA introduced the Crisis Management Information System (CMIS) as a single door for COVID-19-related data management and reporting from all local levels. These local levels operated the CMIS and reported information related to available health infrastructure or facilities, migrants and their management, quarantine and isolation management, relief distribution, etc. The CMIS was expected to be used in decision-making in responding to a pandemic like COVID-19 and other disasters.

The study team observed that all local levels were well informed about the CMIS. However, they did not update it with the COVID-19 information as frequently as needed. The information technology section of Manahari reported that the health section was responsible for collecting all pandemic-related data. Ineffective coordination between the two meant that the CMIS data updating had not been carried out even after 1–2 weeks. Further, MOFAGA gradually slowed down its follow-up on updating the CMIS. Currently, only Pokhara Metropolitan City updates the CMIS on deaths (every 2 days). Hence, local levels are gradually weakening on updating the CMIS and using its data in decision-making to respond to the pandemic. The data fields of the CMIS do not cover other disasters, so it will have to be enhanced and upgraded to make it a single platform for collecting and managing all disaster- and pandemic-related data.

---

[12]   These equipment include rope, picks, sickles, tubes, tarpaulins, trucks, tractors, JCBs/bulldozers, a fire brigade, ambulances, etc.

3. Risks and Challenges

Managing the impacts of the pandemic was a challenging task. Food distribution was entirely unanticipated, and all three tiers of government were not ready for such a long period of lockdown. Below, the risks and challenges involved in addressing the food requirements of vulnerable people are described in detail.

1. Selection of eligible and/or vulnerable households. Even though the Ministry of Federal Affairs and General Administration (MOFAGA) circulated a guideline on providing food relief to vulnerable people, the selection of eligible households remained a challenge for the local levels. As the data profile maintained at the local levels was not sufficient for selecting the poor and vulnerable households, there was a risk of overlooking the needs of such groups. On the other hand, as most local levels formed and activated ward-level committees involving all-party representatives to finalize the list of vulnerable people, the chances of them favoring their voters while selecting families or people eligible for food relief were minimized.

2. Considering migrant workers and students in the food distribution. Collecting information on migrant workers and students from other districts was difficult in city areas like Dhangadi, Pokhara, and Surkhet. Local people demanded food from the local levels using the required documents. In the case of migrant workers, it took longer to verify identity cards and legal documents in making municipal decisions to support them and provide food relief. The study shows that migrant workers were of second priority for the local levels even though they were in a deeper crisis.

3. Redirection of the development budget toward relief distribution. As demand for food from the poor and vulnerable people rose, the regular budgets and disaster management funds of the local levels were insufficient to maintain food supply. As such, they established a single basket fund (the COVID-19 Fund) to collect resources from the federal and provincial governments and the nongovernment sector. In addition, most local levels had no option except to transfer their development budget to the food relief fund to address the food demands of vulnerable people. This was an enabling provision that helped the local levels continue providing food relief for a longer period as necessary.

4. Fiduciary issues. The study team assessed the fiduciary issues of food relief expenditure. Overall, internal control practices were found to be weak in all selected municipalities. They had failed to establish a budgetary control system and established procurement procedures had been relaxed at all local levels during the pandemic.

5. Coordination and mobilization of nongovernment organizations and the private sector. As a result of restrictions on mobility and people's fear of going out, the role of NGOs and CBOs was limited to relief material distribution and providing support for monitoring. A study report published by the NGO Federation of Nepal also mentions that receiving a travel pass from government authorities was the main challenge in the pandemic response and relief distribution. An NGO representative, a journalist, and a Red Cross representative revealed that local-level efforts to coordinate with the nongovernment sector were not adequate in the majority of cases.

6. Monitoring and assurance of food quality. Local levels did not use a third-party mechanism for monitoring food distribution. In most cases, those responsible for selecting eligible households and distributing food were themselves involved in monitoring. As such, there was a risk of ineffective monitoring leading to the distribution of low-quality food. Respondents in Dhangadi highlighted that substandard food items distributed to vulnerable people were returned to the local level. A case filed with the Commission for the Investigation of Abuse of Authority regarding the procurement of low-quality grain is now under investigation.

7. Addressing the grievances of vulnerable people. Local levels had no formal mechanisms to address complaints received from beneficiaries. Only Pokhara established a hotline service to receive hardships and grievances. Other local levels received grievances verbally and tried to resolve them. The study team did not observe any record of receiving and resolving grievances from the poor and vulnerable people. As mobility was restricted during the lockdown, there was a risk of beneficiaries not being able to come to register their grievances with their local government.

8. Sufficiency of food relief for poor and vulnerable people. The study showed that the food distributed for poor and vulnerable people was sufficient for 1–2 weeks across the sampled local levels. There were very few cases of local levels providing food repeatedly. As the lockdown lasted 3–4 months, depending on the severity of the pandemic in the locality, there was a high risk of insufficiency of food relief to the poor and vulnerable people.

4. Conclusion

Based on the findings, the key concluding remarks of this study are as follows.

1. **Identification of eligible households for food relief.** Mobility restrictions during the lockdown severely disturbed people's ability to earn and procure essential commodities. Households headed by women, PWDs, primary food producers, daily wage earners, migrant workers, and workers in the informal sector suffered hardships. MOFAGA defined vulnerable people under its Module for Food Relief for Vulnerable and Poor People. Provinces also developed legislation on managing relief work during the lockdown. local levels did not follow the guidelines strictly to standardize a distribution system applicable to all local levels. The discrepancies relate mainly to (i) failure to properly review previous policies and regulations before establishing new standards, (ii) non-incorporation of current practices, and (iii) an emphasis on the ad hoc creation of untested standards. TDOs, FCHVs, CBOs, women, and social workers were not properly represented in selecting the poor and vulnerable people. Although elected representatives were on the selection committees, this arrangement was not sufficient to recognize the needs of the poor and vulnerable people.

2. **Identifying and addressing specific needs.** In addition to the overall food support to unorganized occupational groups, local levels identified and addressed specific needs for nutritious food of pregnant and lactating women, PWDs, single women, and persons in ill-health. This boosted morale among those from the vulnerable communities and among isolated and quarantined people. Local levels engaged local partners, including NGOs, CBOs, and the private sector, to address social protection issues. This type of support is crucial in disaster and pandemic situations. MOFAGA issued a circular to all local governments to provide necessary relief materials to families and groups requiring special protection. Some local levels also prepared guidelines to address these burning issues. However, in the absence of commonly applicable standards, there is always the possibility of excluding the needy if they are not represented properly.

3. **Strengthening the participation of women and the marginalized in the selection of beneficiaries and the distribution of food.** Women's participation in the selection of beneficiaries and food distribution during the lockdown period was satisfactory. However, their mobility was somewhat limited in the rural context as a result of gender stereotypes. Women often became the sole providers and caregivers in their households. Nevertheless, in terms of providing support voluntarily, women from different segments, including FCHVs; elected officials; representatives of political parties, CBOs, mothers' groups, and TDOs; health and security personnel; teachers; and municipal staff, were found to be very effective. The participation of women and people from various beneficiary groups is also very useful when handling grievances in the communities and in quarantine and isolation centers.

4. **Mechanism for reporting and addressing domestic violence and gender-based violence during crisis.** Men, women, boys, girls, elderly people, and PWDs can experience domestic violence and gender-based violence (GBV) of

varying degrees of intensity and impact. Although several cases may have occurred, only a few were found to have been registered.[13]

The majority of the local levels have not ventured toward adopting the digitization of information even in normal situations. The failure of the local levels to maintain relevant data hinders the follow-up and resolution of domestic violence and GBV cases. Delays owe mainly to (i) limited trained staff to handle cases at the ward level; (ii) women following a culture of silence by not taking cases for further discussion, mediation, and referral; and (iii) judicial committee heads having multiple responsibilities and limited opportunity to resolve such cases. Generally, cases are addressed through a cross-sectional approach covering safety and security, health services, psychosocial counseling, legal services, and logistics support. These services were difficult to arrange during lockdown, especially with no virtual work environment culture.

5. **Resource management.** Following the issuance of the COVID-19 Infection Prevention Control and Treatment Fund Operational Guideline by the federal government in March 2020, all local levels established a COVID-19 Fund for pandemic response. The sources were (i) internal resources of the local levels; (ii) transfers from the federal and provincial governments; and (iii) contributions from the private sector, NGOs, and individuals. Budgetary support from the federal government was nominal in the total resources of each fund.

In some cases, individuals, including municipal staff and local representatives, contributed to the fund, demonstrating their humanity and accountability to fellow citizens. The nine studied local levels spent 37.16% on food relief out of the total available NRs282.7 million in their funds.

6. **Procurement of goods and quality of food.** Six of the nine studied local levels adopted a direct purchase method for procuring food items. They claimed during the discussion that the prices paid for the food items were competitive. Regarding procurement, local levels adopted two different approaches: (i) ward offices procuring food and the municipal office reimbursing them, and (ii) municipal offices procuring and delivering to each ward as per demand. Constraints faced during procurement included reluctance to open shops, low food supply in the locality, price hikes, and unknown quantities of food stock at the local level. These constraints significantly affected the purchase of food for distribution. Some local levels purchased food from the government-owned Food Management and Trade Company, the Salt Trading Corporation, and local cooperatives, which may have promoted efficient and transparent food procurement.

Municipal or ward staff and elected representatives monitored the quality of the food items before dispatching them to the distribution centers or to vulnerable people. Monitoring methods involved only visual observations and obtaining feedback from beneficiaries. The best practice by one local level was a technical quality test of food items by the Food Technology and Quality Control Office.

7. **Monitoring and beneficiary feedback mechanism.** Local levels monitored food distribution through field visits to observe distribution centers and through discussions directly with beneficiaries. The study revealed that there was no third-party mechanism to monitor the process of food distribution. In most local levels, those responsible for selecting eligible households and distributing food relief were also involved in monitoring. Monitoring of food distribution was carried out by elected representatives, municipal or ward staff, and municipal and ward-level COVID-19 control and management committees. In a few cases, local levels involved media persons and representatives of civil society, which added value

---

[13] During lockdown, the judiciary remained closed and judiciary committees at the local levels were not adequately resourced and capacitated.

in gaining broader support from the community level. The study showed that distributed food was of better quality in places where the local levels had ensured the participation of civil society.

In general, practices for the formal registration and resolution of grievances and feedback were not in place; however, Pokhara had established a hotline service for the reporting of grievances and other hardships faced by people as a result of mobility restrictions and/or lockdown.[14] In other cases, mobility restrictions meant that people could not register grievances and hardships with the nearest government office or local level. Grievances were largely related to the eligibility of households for food relief support. Local levels tried their best to resolve verbal grievances by mobilizing additional food support.

8. **Governance and accountability.** Significant numbers of local levels prepared food distribution reports and disclosed these on their websites. As a good practice, one local level also disseminated ward-wise expenditure at the TDO level and received feedback. Local levels did not make any serious attempt to conduct a social or public audit of food support activity expenditure nor mobilize civil society to ensure accountability in the food relief distribution process.

9. **Coordination and mobilization of the private sector and development partners.** Local levels formally requested the private sector, NGOs, individuals, and civil society to complement government efforts to provide food relief to vulnerable people during the lockdown. Local levels successfully collected support from these nonstate actors. The private sector was more willing to contribute to direct relief programming than NGOs, which provided support through their regular project activities and mobilized immediately

through humanitarian assistance. Some local levels were aware that their efforts to work with the private sector and NGOs were inadequate. However, with some exceptions, local levels coordinated in a timely manner with the private sector, NGOs, individuals, and civil society in adopting a single door policy to provide relief support.

10. **Disaster- and pandemic-responsive planning of the local levels.** All local levels have local disaster management committees, which performed effectively during the pandemic. Ward-level disaster management committees were formed and operationalized for a short period during the pandemic. Although all local levels have disaster management funds to mitigate the impacts of disasters and pandemics, these have some limitations in terms of allocating sufficient resources without support from external entities. Local levels are in the process of preparing disaster fund mobilization guidelines. The guideline of one local level explicitly mentions the use of the fund for providing food relief to victims of disasters.

Regarding the safety, search, and rescue of survivors of disasters, local levels coordinate with both the Nepal Police and the Armed Police. Some local levels provide search and rescue tools to police offices. Metropolitan and submetropolitan municipalities are better equipped than rural municipalities, but they still do not have sufficient tools and equipment to respond to disasters. Although some local levels have groups of trained volunteers for immediate response, all local levels have inadequate human resources dedicated to disaster response and management. Local levels had minimal use of digital information systems during the pandemic.

11. **Updating of the Crisis Management Information System and its utilization.** CMIS data were useful

---

14 Some of the reported issues include people reaching their destination; transport access to health facilities for the needy; meeting food and transport requirements for migrants and students; medicine supplies for regular medicine users, etc.

not only for the local levels but also for both provincial and federal governments. Local levels compiled COVID-19 information and reported this to MOFAGA. Local levels have designated information technology officers with multiple responsibilities in disaster and pandemic data compilation and reporting. However, local levels have yet to create an enabling environment for information management and a dedicated information technology section or unit. CMIS data were not fully and effectively used for planning, policy formulation, and monitoring at all levels.

5. Recommendations

Based on the findings, the study has some policy recommendations for the local levels to effectively plan and execute relief programs in the event of future crises.

1. **Strengthen the database of the poor, the marginalized, and the vulnerable households, and design and operationalize appropriate targeting mechanisms for identifying beneficiaries at the local levels.** Intersector coordination can be established to avoid thematic and geographical overlaps, harmonize implementation procedures, and effectively utilize available funds to address social protection issues. A range of approaches for selecting beneficiaries can be adopted (either geographical or household targeting), drawing lessons from past initiatives. The distribution policies of the governments in the rural and urban areas need to be considered differently in the future and support should be provided accordingly.[15]

2. **Address the specific needs of pregnant and lactating women, persons with disabilities, single women, and persons in ill-health to reduce vulnerability.** MOFAGA should prepare a national policy and standardize common practices of the local levels to address the specific needs of vulnerable people. In coordination with stakeholders, including the private sector and civil society, local levels should design nutritious food content to address the specific needs of pregnant and lactating women, PWDs, the elderly, children under 5 years of age, and persons in ill-health, thereby reducing the extent of their marginalization during the time of such vulnerability. Local levels should explore and adopt alternative means of food support during crisis, such as food-for-work, cash-for-work, and cash transfers or cash vouchers, as deemed appropriate.

3. **Design and implement capacity development measures (institutional, technical, and managerial) at all functional levels, including for municipal and ward-level disaster management committees.** Promote participation and strengthen the capacity of women and the marginalized community in the selection of beneficiaries and the distribution of relief materials. Local levels should strengthen the capacity of existing mothers' groups, FCHVs, social workers, women's associations or networks, women cooperatives, and women-led CBOs and mobilize them to monitor gender and inclusion biases in access to services.[16]

4. **Strengthen the operationalization of judicial committees.** Local levels should establish proper mechanisms for the effective operationalization of judicial committees by mobilizing trained staff, hiring legal domestic violence and/or GBV experts, digitizing information with confidentiality, raising awareness at the community level, mobilizing a local GBV network, and addressing cases and providing referral services. Legal services need to be fully activated during crisis to handle the GBV cases.

5. **Strengthen the capacity of the local levels to manage and mobilize resources.** Local levels

---

[15] In urban areas, a cash-for-work modality may be fitting; whereas, in rural areas, food-for-work may be more appropriate.

[16] Gender-specific needs and traditional work patterns need to be recognized.

should allocate sufficient resources to disaster management funds to address possible disasters in the future. They should coordinate with the private sector, NGOs, and civil society to collect additional resources and mitigate crisis impact. Such a mechanism will ensure broader recognition and support from the community, bringing more transparency to fund collection and management.

6. **Strengthen procurement capacity and food quality control.** The provisions in public procurement rules regarding "procurement under special circumstances" (such as pandemics, floods, earthquakes, and other disasters) should be made more specific. Contract information, including rates and grading of food items, should be disseminated on the internet. Local levels should strengthen and operationalize their procurement units, supported by macroeconomic experts and procurement specialists. They should prioritize government-owned entities and local cooperatives when purchasing food and other items.

7. **Establish a separate monitoring system and grievance redressal mechanism.** Local levels should establish a third-party monitoring system, with the representation of local security offices, CSOs, the private sector, and the Red Cross, to monitor the selection of vulnerable people and the distribution of relief and to track the proper use of relief support. Similarly, local levels need to operationalize a grievance redressal mechanism to register and resolve grievances and address hardships faced by women, poor people, and vulnerable people.

8. **Strengthen the capacity of municipal and ward-level disaster management committees.** Local levels should constitute a dedicated disaster management section with trained human resources, supported by volunteers for immediate response. Municipal and ward-level disaster management committees should be strengthened and activated throughout the year for necessary preparedness and response during disasters and pandemics.

6. List of Reference Documents and Websites

Gautam, Dhruba. 2020. *The COVID-19 Crisis in Nepal: Coping Crackdown Challenges—Key Initiatives and Measures to Move Forward.* Kathmandu: National Disaster Risk Reduction Centre Nepal. https://www.alnap.org/help-library/the-covid-19-crisis-in-nepal-coping-crackdown-challenges.

Government of Nepal, Ministry of Federal Affairs and General Administration (MOFAGA). Circulars to the Local Levels. https://www.mofaga.gov.np/news-notice/1807 (in Nepali), and https://www.mofaga.gov.np/news-notice/1811 (in Nepali).

Government of Nepal, MOFAGA. Crisis Management Information System (CMIS). https://cmis.mofaga.gov.np/.

Government of Nepal, MOFAGA. 2019. Sample Relief Standard for Informal Sector Workers and Destitute. www.mofaga.gov.np/news-notice/1831 (in Nepali).

Government of Nepal, MOFAGA. 2020. Rapid Need Assessment and COVID-19 Responsive Planning Framework (Sample).

Government of Nepal, Nepal Law Commission. 2017. *Federal Disaster Risk Reduction and Management Act 2017.* Kathmandu.

International Organization for Migration. 2020. *Rapid Assessment on Impacts of COVID-19 on Returnee Migrants and Responses of Local Governments of Nepal.* Kathmandu. https://reliefweb.int/report/nepal/rapid-assessment-impacts-covid-19-returnee-migrants-and-responses-local-governments.

Madhesh Provincial Office, Chief Minister and Council of Ministers. 2019. Relief Distribution (Standards and Monitoring) Guideline for COVID-19-Affected Workers, Poor, and Vulnerable Farmers . Janakpur.

NGO Federation of Nepal. 2021. *Role of Social Institution Amidst COVID-19 Pandemic—A Rapid Assessment.* Kathmandu.

UNICEF Nepal. 2020. *Child and Family Tracker: Tracking the Socio-Economic Impact of COVID-19 on Children and Families in Nepal.* A PowerPoint presentation of the 2nd Monthly Household Survey July 2020 Findings. Lalitpur. https://www.unicef.org/nepal/media/9971/file/Child_and_Family_Tracker_-_July_2020_Findings.pdf.

World Food Programme. 2020. *Nepal COVID-19 Economic Vulnerability Index: Overview and Technical Guidance.* Lalitpur. https://docs.wfp.org/api/documents/WFP-0000117595/download/.

World Vision International Nepal. 2021. *Multi-Sectoral Impact of the COVID-19 Second Wave in Nepal 2021: Key Findings from a Rapid Assessment/Household Survey.* Lalitpur. https://www.wvi.org/publications/policy-paper/nepal/multi-sectoral-impact-covid-19-second-wave-nepal-2021.

Websites of the Nine Sampled Local Levels:

1.	Bideha Municipality. https://bidehamun.gov.np/

2.	Birendranagar Municipality. https://birendranagarmun.gov.np/ne

3.	Dhangadi Submetropolitan City. https://dhangadhimun.gov.np/

4.	Janakpurdham Submetropolitan City. https://janakpurmun.gov.np/ne

5.	Manahari Rural Municipality. https://manaharimun.gov.np/

6.	Pokhara Metropolitan City. www.pokharamun.gov.np/

7.	Rambha Rural Municipality. https://rambhamun.gov.np/

8.	Rangeli Municipality. https://rangelimun.gov.np/ne

9.	Suddodhan Rural Municipality. https://shuddhodhanmunrupandehi.gov.np/

Disaster Fund Mobilization Guidelines of the Local Levels:

1.	Disaster Fund Mobilization Guideline 2018 of Janakpurdham Submetropolitan City

2.	Disaster Fund Mobilization and Management Guideline 2018 of Manahari Rural Municipality

3.	Disaster Fund Mobilization Guideline 2018 of Pokhara Metropolitan City

Disaster Risk Reduction and Management Act of the Local Levels:

1.	Disaster Risk Reduction and Management Act 2018 of Manahari Rural Municipality

2.	Disaster Risk Reduction and Management Act 2019 of Suddodhan Rural Municipality

3.	Disaster Risk Reduction and Management Act 2020 of Pokhara Metropolitan City

Local Level Reports on Relief Distribution

1.	A Rapid Assessment of Relief Distribution Effectiveness, 2020—A Study of Pokhara Metropolitan City

2.	Birendranagar Municipality, Lockdown Relief Distribution Management Program Report 2077

www.ingramcontent.com/pod-product-compliance
Lightning Source LLC
Chambersburg PA
CBHW042035220326
41599CB00045BA/7426